MONARCH ILLUSTRATED GUIDE TO

VARMINT HUNTING

by Chuck Riekert

MONARCH PRESS

Cover and Text Illustrations by Leonard B. Cole

Published by
MONARCH PRESS, a Simon & Schuster Division of
Gulf & Western Corporation
Simon & Schuster Building
1230 Avenue of the Americas
New York, N.Y. 10020

ISBN: 0-671-18766-X

Manufactured in the United States of America

Contents

	Introduction	5
ONE	Safety	7
TWO	The King of Avian Targets	9
THREE	The Canny Canines	23
FOUR	The Winged Piranhas	43
FIVE	Fang and Beak	53
SIX	The Varmint Villager	71
SEVEN	The Sly Ones	81
EIGHT	Beak and Talons	95
NINE	The Wild Cats	105
TEN	The Power Mower	121
ELEVEN	Starlings and Sparrows	135
TWELVE	Other Furred Pests	141
THIRTEEN	Sighting-in Your Rifle	155
FOURTEEN	Shotgun Hints	157
FIFTEEN	Varminting Accessories	165

"Please, Lord, let me kill clean,
but if I can not kill clean,
please let me miss clean!"

Introduction

The calendar tells you that the hunting season is officially over. Therefore, as a law-abiding citizen you dutifully put away your guns until next autumn. In so doing, you are missing out on a most productive and rewarding shooting sport . . . Varmint Hunting.

Very few large game animals provide the test of your shooting skills as do the smaller, hard-to-hit varmints. As an example, prairie dogs are shot at distances of anywhere between 100 and 300 yards. At best they provide an extremely small target and a kill ratio of one out of three attempts is considered very good indeed. Please note that this target is almost motionless and still is most difficult to nail. Another illustration of formidable shooting problems is presented by the coyote. Here again you will be shooting at ranges of 300 yards or better, only this time your quarry is moving, and moving in a somewhat erratic pattern. No place here for . . . the once-in-a-while shooter.

These are merely two of the many varmints we will cover in detail in this book. We shall attempt to delineate in the ensuing chapters the How, When, Where and With-What to successfully hunt your game. For example: how to identify your quarry; how to accurately gauge shooting distances; how to adjust for and solve ballistics problems; where, when and how to hunt; specific characteristics of the game (where it lives, when it moves from place to place, its feeding habits, when and where it rests, etc.). Here is a complete how-to guide to the hunting of every recognized species of varmint.

It is an acknowledged fact that varmint hunting keeps the eyes and reflexes in trim and provides *year-round* practice in bagging game at bragging range with light gun and fitted scope.

Varminting is rarely restricted by game laws in that it curtails the numbers of harmful vermin (varmints) that prey on man's valuable crops and wildlife.

This guidebook can provide the means of turning a neophyte hunter into a fine, conservation and ecology-minded sportsman.

The photography is by Jean and Ray Shapiro.

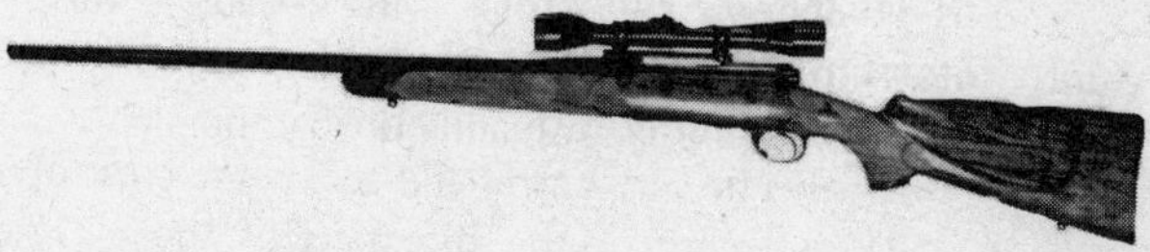

Chapter 1
Safety

Anytime a man starts out to do anything, part of his preparation must, or should, include safety guides. Before driving his car, he should be sure his tires and brakes are in tip-top shape; he should know that the horn and the lights and windshield wipers work at proper efficiency; and as important as everything else, he, himself, should be in the proper frame of mind and body so that he can concentrate on the task at hand properly. If he's starting out to paint his house, he must be sure that the ladder he is going to use is sturdy enough to sustain him, that it rests squarely on the ground so as not to slip while he's on the top rung, etc. In other words, there are safety rules for everything, even to the relatively simple task of crossing the street.

So it is with the handling of a gun. The "Ten Commandments" of gun safety appear in practically all gun and sporting publications. Unfortunately, they are sometimes overlooked or deliberately ignored, much like their biblical counterparts. It is this flagrant, and stupid, disobedience of the rules of gun safety that causes the accidents we all read about in the newspapers. You know . . . the tragic slaying of a friend or relative by the fellow cleaning his "unloaded" gun; the senseless killing of a child by his playmate who found his father's loaded revolver laying around the house carelessly; the hunter bending over his rifle as he cleans it against a tree trunk and cleanly blows his head off.

Each of these ten rules has a sound and reasonable purpose . . . to allow you and all others like you to enjoy your hunting and to continue enjoying it without tragic interruption. They are herewith listed. Read and heed them most carefully:

1. Treat *every* gun with the respect due a loaded gun.
2. Guns carried into camp or home, or when otherwise not in use, must *always* be unloaded.
3. *Always* be sure barrel and action are clear of obstruction.
4. *Always* control the direction of the muzzle, even if you stumble.
5. *Be sure* of your target before you pull the trigger.
6. *Never* point a gun at anything you do not want to shoot.
7. Unattended guns *must* be unloaded.
8. *Never* climb a tree or fence or jump a ditch with a loaded gun.
9. *Never* shoot a bullet at a flat, hard surface or the surface of water.
10. *Always* avoid alcoholic drinks before or during shooting.

True, some of these rules duplicate, repeat and overlap others. But they are all so very important for your own and everybody else's well-being that they can stand much repetition. To sum them all up, always remember that a gun is a dangerous, deadly weapon. So, BE CAREFUL AND THOUGHTFUL.

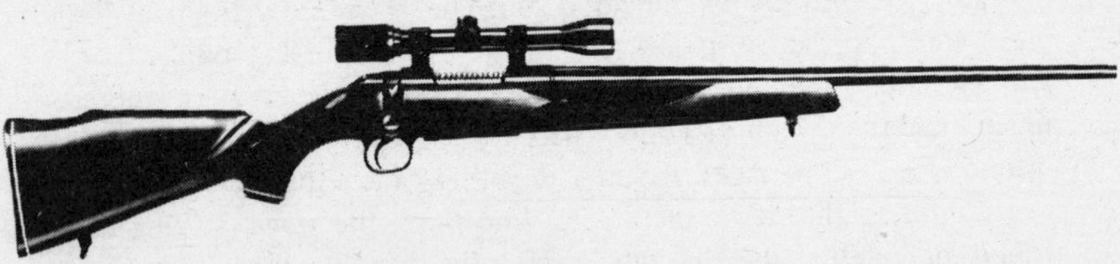

Chapter 2 The King of Avian Targets

The crow reigns supreme as the most sought-after prize by varmint hunters everywhere. It is a fact that no other quarry is hunted as relentlessly as are these ebon-hued gangsters. They are number one on the list which includes any and all game pests on land, water or in the air.

The reasons are manifold, a prime factor being that these birds are to be found in nearly every sector of the North American continent, with the exception of extremely high mountainous country and truly arid desert regions. These areas are avoided to ensure a continuance of the species. Crows cannot tolerate the extremely high temperatures of the Southwestern badlands as these barren stretches provide little or no shade and the heat is debilitating to the birds. Conversely, the freezing temperatures common to the high-country often prove destructive to the crow eggs. Another factor for the avoidance of these areas is the scarcity of a readily available food source. This becomes a most vital reason for concern during the period of nesting. It is during this season that crows require a diet rich in protein and normally this nutriment is most plentiful at this time.

No doubt this is what causes these black-winged bandits to prey so relentlessly on the eggs of other birds. They are indiscriminate in their tastes. Quite commonly they will strip bare the nests of any and all birds that are in the process of incubating eggs. This is especially true should the nest owners be unable to fend off their predations.

Crows will readily assault the nests of waterfowl that have nested on the shoreline or in the water, as well as songbird nests and those of upland game birds.

However, once the young of such birds are born, the raiding goes on at an even more furious pace. Now the crows have young of their own and the family needs are greater than ever. So, the adult crows kill the young of their victim species wherever they find them unguarded, then take the tender meat to their nests for their own newborn. Most of the time, the young victims attract fatal crow attention by "cheeping" for parental attention.

Technically known as "simps," a name very aptly applied, the crow young grow at a fantastic pace and are soon ready to follow their parents in attacks on the earliest of berry, fruit, vegetable and grain crops. The parent birds, now somewhat freed of the job of finding food, go into the moult.

Young crows do not respond to calling too avidly at this time of the year. Nor do their parents. The elders' moulting plumage is quite worn-looking and they have poor control of their flight. It is not at all unusual for family flocks to fly away from areas where the caller-hunter sets up a hopeful clamor. Crow hunting then drops to its lowest point of productivity during the entire year.

In certain areas of the country the crow remains on in copious quantities even during the time of nesting and wintering. Therefore, hunting limitations are not to be attributed to the crow, rather to the time and effort the hunter can expend in seeking out his quarry. There is, of course, the financial aspect to be considered, specifically how much money he can afford to expend in his pursuit of crows.

Another reason for their popularity as targets is that crows are a truly hardy breed. While they don't particularly enjoy it, they can endure extreme weather fantastically well, as long as they can find food and shelter.

Also, these creatures are basically targets for shotgun. That means they have to be lured to a short range of 40 to 50 yards. There are also such other requirements as: good calling, which requires a certain degree of musical knowledge, a retentive memory of the effective calls plus the ability to reproduce them in a satisfactory manner; discipline on the part of the hunter in the blind so that he doesn't frighten (or spook) the targets until they are within shooting range; almost superb marksmanship to adjust quickly and accurately to the great variety of shots they present; and a full knowledge and awareness of weather conditions, flight patterns, and the wariness which these intelligent birds own in almost unlimited quantities.

RECORD CALLER

Crow calling sounds

CROW CALL

On the subject of calling, it's a good idea to listen to live birds as much as possible so as to perfect realistic imitations. There are a number of call and decoy makers who offer crow-calling recordings for sale. Either way, perfect a number of calls because there are many different caws in the crow language, depending on whether a bird is feeding, fighting, screaming for help or just plain gossiping.

The neophyte crow hunter really need master only three basic calls. The first of these is the "distress" call. The crow sounds this call as a wail for help from all crows within hearing. Without a doubt, this is the most important, most heavily used call. It is used to start practically every crow flight over the hidden gunners. As many as 75 percent of all crows killed are shot over this one call.

You must employ the diaphragm as the control for ejecting air from the lungs, and the vocal chords as a tuning fork augmenting the vibration of the call's reed. Continuously say "oooh," while calling, strongly enough so the reed is in full vibration. The best calling is done in a rapid tempo. This call demands help—lots of help and right now! Crows that respond come zooming in to the battle so fast that, before they know it, they're over the waiting gunners. Under perfect conditions, they will keep coming even after they identify armed hunters. They're so completely fooled they seemingly can't believe their own eyes. In calling, be careful not to use calling that is too short and choppy. You see, crows have a danger signal which is given in this manner. Therefore, you might well alert crows to potential danger and defeat your own purpose.

The second call the beginning crow hunter should master is the come-back or return call. This can best be described as sounding like someone yelling, "Hey, hey; look here!" The first two sounds are somewhat short and choppy; the last two are relatively longer in duration and smoother. None of the four parts of this call is held quite as long as the wailing notes of the distress call, but they are just as commanding. Crows interpret this call as the voice of some comrade who has discovered something new and interesting and is screaming for all his buddies to come over and see what he found. The main purpose of this call is to get back crows that have flown away from the gunners. It's also used to bring in crows who seem reluctant to answer to the distress call. It is a call whose effects have to be seen to be believed. This particular call is used quite sparingly. Generally, it is used twice in rapid succession, then back to the distress call. But if a really intelligent crow warily stays out there and refuses to be lured into a headlong approach by the distress call, it can be used every time the crow turns to fly away. Then resume the distress call as it turns back, and so on. There have been cases where a single crow was held within 75 to 100 yards for several minutes by such means. Finally, it seems to give up playing it safe and comes in to join its less wary friends—on the ground.

The third call is a duplicate of the "mourning" call crows use when one of their chums seems wounded and they're sympathizing with it. This sound is somewhat lower-pitched than the distress call, nowhere near as desperate in tone. It's almost as though the crows were saying, "Gee, buddy, what's wrong with you?" One reason why crippled crows shouldn't be allowed to wander out to the leeward side of a blind is that they attract the mourners. Since the purpose of crow calling is to keep a stream of fresh targets coming toward the blind-hidden hunters, such delays can cause a ganging-up of mourning crows over a cripple. Then, when they finally come in answer to the distress call, they may come in flocks too large to be efficiently handled. Large numbers of targets, some of which are almost certain to sight the gunners and take fright, often lower the potential kill. It's much better to have a steady stream of targets, dispose of one small batch at a time, and then turn your attention to the next onslaught. So the mourning call should be used sparingly.

It is far better to remove the cause for its need during a slowdown in the action. But should a few crows somehow slide in and start mourning over some wounded birds, they must be moved out of there in a hurry. The caller first mourns with them, then lets loose with a shocking spasm of distress calling to clear the flight bottleneck.

This wary bird is discernible enough to spot a blind that seems contrived. No matter how carefully the structure is assembled, if it's not put together with material common to the area, he will sense danger because of this construction error. Also, make certain that the blind is adequate enough in size to fully conceal the hunters within its confines.

There are numerous methods of constructing a blind; however, the most important factor to remember is, how its occupants behave. Any overt movement, any unnatural gesture, any sudden motion will certainly be spotted by the black marauders and result in a fly-off.

Strangely enough, the sound of gunfire or the sight of their comrades falling seems to have no hand in frightening off the remaining crows. However, the sight of a human in the vicinity will indeed serve to frighten them away.

Many times it is quite possible to down the point bird in the group and if the following birds perceive no motion from the blind a goodly number of the following crows can still be called back into killing range. It is for this reason that a greater kill can be accomplished by the solitary hunter than when more than one individual is in the blind. It is quite obvious that two or more persons will find it exceedingly difficult to remain absolutely still. One of the hunters is almost certain to make an involuntary, alarming gesture at an inopportune moment and in so doing, spoil the fly-over.

Certainly the prudent use of good calls and the clever placement of decoys will serve you well, but all these will come to naught if you don't remain completely hidden.

Here a repetition of warning *cannot be overly stressed.* Once again, a word of caution to the wise . . . make certain that no alert member of the flock discerns any suspicious movement or alien shape. Should this happen, you can be sure that he will remain out of range, and through his ability to communicate with his fellows he will sound the alarm that will be noted by every crow in the vicinity.

The primary way of hunting these canny gangsters is to shoot them where they roost. These arch villains of the sportsmen's world fly far and wide to find food, leaving early in the morning and winging back to their place of rest in the early evening. A knowledge of crow habits and painstaking scouting of the countryside, plus careful observation of where the flight lanes come together, is required to locate a crow roost. Just finding a great congregation of birds doesn't necessarily mean you've found a roost. Many times, they will fly to a common gathering place from which they will send out scouts to make sure that all is safe before they approach their nightly resting place. So be careful and be patient. Because once you do discover the roost, you're in business.

While crows can perform acrobatics in flight, they are not strong fliers. This is a fact you can put to great advantage. The light weight of their bodies and their large areas of wing and tail feathers cause them to have some difficulty controlling themselves when flying with the wind or across it. When flying with a tail wind, they choose to stay high in the air, as if fearing a collision or a crash landing. However, flying directly into the wind, he has perfect control over his movement and he is not the least bit reluctant to come down closer to the ground. So, a hunter who is shooting near a roost should set up his blind where the birds will be able to fly directly into the wind to answer the call. The birds will oftentimes make several passes over the blind, and this is important. It enables you to be picky about which shots to attempt. You don't always have much choice about which individual birds in a flock to try for, or when to fire. But remember that birds coming in on a direct line toward you are the easiest to kill.

Besides a well-constructed, well-hidden blind and a perfected set of crow calls, a goodly number of well-placed decoys will help the hunter pile up a high score of crow kills. Naturally, there is no better decoy than the real thing. Therefore, when you've had a fairly successful day of crow hunting, save all the crows you've killed if you plan to shoot again the next day. You can spread these executed predators in nearby trees, on rail fences, or stake them out in an open field. Do this and you're almost certain to double the previous day's kill.

It becomes a matter of personal preference among varminters as to which firearm to use. There are the purists who feel that only those birds killed with a rifle should be counted in their overall score. Others

OWL AS CROW DECOY

CROW

COYOTE

RED FOX

GREAT HORNED OWL

who feel that the only good crow is a dead crow, will tell you that the shotgun is the best medicine to cure the common crow. Very few riflemen can claim a positive crow kill of 300 birds during one year's shooting. However, many scatter-gunners rack up fantastic scores. A large number of them approach or even exceed 1,500 kills over a twelve-month span of time. Taking into consideration how many crows this would total in a normal lifetime of shooting, the gross figure becomes staggering. Yet there seems to be nothing doubtful about such claims.

A gun with modified or improved choke seems to work best. It is a matter of proper timing and accurate lead that posts the most impressive number of defunct crows. If you are after a great number of kills,

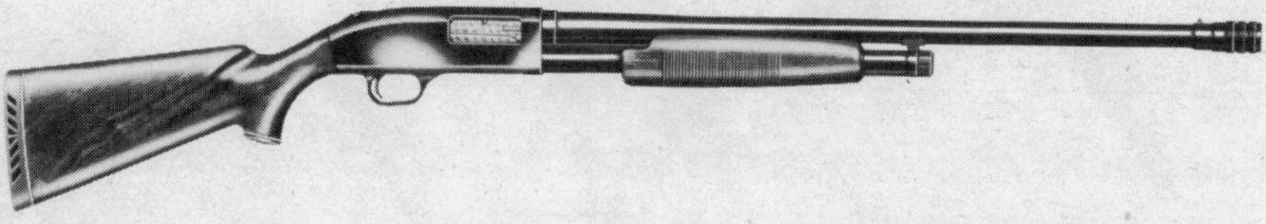

MOSSBERG MODEL 500K

it is best to use either a pump action or autoloading gun, as you will have the opportunity in most instances to get off as many as five shots when a flock comes in, in answer to your call.

Crow hunting presents an ideal opportunity to burn up all those odd loads left over from the regular hunting season. It is immaterial whether you use No. 4, 5 or 6 shot since the only results you are after is decimation of the crow population. Certainly you're not concerned whether or not the birds' carcasses are damaged in the process. Not too many people eat crow.

However, many purists stay within the No. 7½ or No. 8 shot range while others will go as high as No. 9 skeet loads. Seemingly, those using smaller pellets reap the most birds; the reason being, they feel it uneconomical to waste their efforts and ammunition shooting at extended ranges. Up close, the denser patterns prove more deadly.

With all these items considered, the one most important factor regarding ammunition is . . . quantity. Have enough on hand for a prolonged shoot. There are very few things more thwarting than to be confronted with an aerial armada of crows and find yourself out of ammunition.

Chapter 3
The Canny Canines

In appearance, the coyote can be said to resemble a dog. But the likeness is only skin-deep, for this wily critter is about as dog-like in attitude as a runaway buzz saw. Due to man's incessant pursuit of him, this varmint has developed into a steel-hard, super-intelligent animal. He has become adept at avoiding his own demise by hunters using poison, traps or firearms. This character is an animal to be reckoned with.

In the early days of our country, the coyote was to be found mostly in the Great Plains area. The two most generally used pronunciations of his name indicate his long lease on the land extending from Canada to Mexico. In the southern tier of that huge tract, mostly settled in those days by Spanish-Mexican peoples, he is called *ki-o-tee;* further north, he is known as the *ki-oat.* Either way, the emphasis is on the first syllable.

During those early days, coyotes used to follow the big gray wolves and great grizzly bears. After these supreme hunter-killers had finished their meal, the coyote would scavenge what was left. Of course, there were times when the grays and grizzlies left nothing but skin and bones. Then the coyote would have to search out the previous day's kill. Since some of those leavings had turned somewhat ripe, coyotes came to accept carrion as readily as they did fresh meat. You see, coyotes would not hesitate to kill jackrabbits, prarie dogs, gophers, etc. But, when they wanted to feast on the bigger, tastier game such as deer, elk or buffalo, they would follow a gray wolf or grizzly, wait for them to make a kill and finish eating their fill.

During the past 150 years, great changes have taken place. Only a comparatively few deer and antelope remain in the Great Plains; the big bison is found only in state and federal game reserves; elk have gone to the mountains further west; gray wolves and grizzly bears are in very small supply between Canada and Mexico. And so, the coyote has extended his range to a really remarkable degree. The shaggy, sharp-featured canines now cover a vast territory stretching from Mexico north into Alaska and across much of Canada. Quite a number of them spread eastward, across the Mississippi, as far as New England. They are found mostly in very rough and broken country or in the timbered mountains.

Along with the change in habitat, coyote nature and food habits have also changed drastically. Due to the extreme hunting pressures that he is forced to live under, the varmint has developed a character which can only be described as skulking and fearful. However, this attitude is only evident in his dealings with humans. Over the years he has become rudely aware that man is his deadly enemy and therefore if he chooses to remain alive, he had best remain out of sight. There is no morsel so tempting, no meal so easy to procure, that will tempt him to remain in an area that carries even the faintest scent of man.

Today's coyote will seldom go near the fresh entrails of any dressed-out big-game kill for quite a time, as long as three days. They've come to know that the innards might be poisoned or that the hunters might be hiding in cover, waiting to shoot them while they scavenge.

With little or none of his earlier carrion providers around, the coyote has turned killer in his own right. He'll still go after a tasty meal of prairie dog and he won't pass up a chance to join his mate in rolling a jackrabbit. Even more to his taste are the bigger and better mountain-country woodchucks. But now, with the gray wolves and grizzly bears no longer bringing down the big game, the coyote has become his own provider by going after his own game.

As noted before, coyotes have mostly left the plains and moved in great numbers to the timbered mountains. There the coyote finds he can conduct his hunting with a certain peace of mind; fewer humans interfering, scenting up the premises, or even loading the uneaten scraps of kills with poisons. These varmints also find the higher elevations offer a more calming and cooler climate during their annual pupping seasons.

Sheepmen swear that coyotes followed their wool-bearing herds to the mountainous summering pastures with malice aforethought. However, the fact is that sheep loss to coyotes is no more serious today than it had been on the plains. While these sheepmen claim that coyotes are ferociously destructive to their herds, beef ranchers don't seem to care one way or the other about coyote control. These differing attitudes are probably based on the naturally different habits of the two forms of livestock. A ewe can easily be frightened. In moments of imminent personal danger, she'll forget all about the romantic notion of mother-love and take off when a coyote attacks. But an adult cow, watching her calf, will give rise to her indignation and put the bum's rush on any critter with fresh veal on his mind.

Also warlike when it comes to defending their ungainly young are elk and moose cows. Deer will do their best to protect their fawns but they're generally no match for a pair of coyotes determined on killing one of the young deer. Antelope, whose young become mobile surprisingly soon after birth, also get help from other does in the area. If they should catch a coyote chasing a kid, they'll often gang up on him, run into him to roll him over, and chop him with their punishing hoofs.

There's another reason that coyotes kill considerably more deer fawns than antelope kids. Does often hide their young and leave them alone for relatively long periods of time. Prowling coyotes that come across such prizes can thus kill them before any defense is possible. Antelope, on the other hand, keep sharp lookouts for any danger threatening their newborn. They move quickly, and often in force, to repel any attacks.

Adult deer and antelope, now, are an entirely different matter. The basically cowardly coyote seldom bothers them except under extreme circumstances. When the ground is covered with deep and crusted snow, these slinking critters can run on top of the crust while the sharp hoofs of their intended victims break through. Running through deep snow that way quickly exhausts the larger game and makes them relatively easy prey for the cunning coyote. These canny canines also take after pregnant does, somehow knowing that these heavily-burdened females are easily exhausted. As noted, these are extreme circumstances. Normally, when food of other kinds is in good supply, such goings-on are kept to a minimum.

Coyotes do have one particularly strange habit. They will store up food in quantity shortly before their pups are born. It has not been established whether this is insurance against a renegade critter hunting alone and unable to supply his mate and her pups, or whether it is a tendency of the animals to have a goodly supply of somewhat ripened carrion on hand. Whatever the reason, coyotes will go on a killing spree at that time of year. These quantity kills, far beyond what the creatures need for their daily feeding, are usually made at considerable distance from the pupping dens and then brought back and left near the dens. Generally, these stockpiles are not used too much, which leads to the thought that they are there merely as insurance against some unpredictable future need for food. Perhaps, the smell naturally emanating from this carrion meat keeps away animals and birds that might otherwise prove dangerous to the expected pups.

Like elk and antelope, coyotes are most protective of their pups. They've been known to kill every rattlesnake within a half-mile of their dens. When it comes to bobcats, coyotes become raging furies if these cats wander within even greater distances of their pups.

When human hunters enter the picture, parent coyotes will often become practically suicidal in trying to draw humans away from their dens. The closer that men approach to the den, the more desperately reckless they become. These animals will draw attention to themselves

by barking and making conspicuous runs in plain sight. Invariably, the coyotes will try to lead the humans away from the den.

Of course, the experienced hunter can judge, by the degree of recklessness shown by the adults, whether or not they're going in the right direction. If the tolling coyotes suddenly disappear, the hunter knows he's been led off on a false scent. A reversal of direction by the hunter will most often bring on a resumption of coyote activity.

If hunters are accompanied by dogs, the adult coyotes try to toll

the dogs off in a sight chase. But any domestic dog that accepts such an invitation to a chase is really asking for king-sized trouble. One coyote will tease him along, seemingly about to be caught, while the mate comes along behind the unwary and soon-to-be unfortunate dog. When they've led the unwitting pooch far enough away from its master, they suddenly turn on him, one from the front and the other from the rear.

Coyote fangs, while fast, are inadequate for one-slash kills. They make up for that lack in quality by quantity delivery on vulnerable targets plus lightning-fast evasion of any retaliatory measures. Any coyote opponent of size, such as a dog, is thus bitten many times, with the fangs penetrating deeply and painfully with each bite.

Any domestic dog that is unfortunate or stupid enough to mix with a pair of pup-defending coyotes finds himself bitten in bursts, often from the rear and in areas he has always regarded private. When he turns to defend such vulnerable and painful targets, he shockingly learns that he isn't nearly fast enough to guard any part of his anatomy. He is engulfed in a world full of flashing fangs, no single one of them deadly but in concert exerting a tremendous drain on his energy, dignity and courage. Big, brave dogs, previously convinced they can swallow alive any coyote they happen to meet, suddenly find themselves helpless in the face of twin-fanged whirlwinds.

If the dog and its slow-footed master have been lured well away from the pup den, this lesson may last anywhere from 10 to 30 seconds . . . unless the poor pooch is somewhat mentally retarded and slow to learn. Then it might take all of two minutes to convince him that he has underestimated his opponents and overestimated his own prowess to an almost fatal degree. Very seldom is the dog fatally injured, but he has a lasting violation of his dignity to prove his misjudgment. Very few dogs come out of such an experience with any high degree of self-confidence.

In areas where coyotes are in abundance, these little wolves will sometimes use these same dog-degrading tactics during the cold weather months, especially if a loud-mouthed domestic is interfering with their hunting. More often than not, they'll do this during the hours of darkness, when man hasn't either the speed afoot or the night vision to back up his best friend. One coyote will lure the dog into a straight-on chase, staying just far enough ahead so a fighting encounter seems only a jump or two away. Meanwhile, the rest of the coyote pack cuts off the dog's retreat.

Then the pooch is given the business. Very often, when caught up in such pack tollings, the dog is lucky to get back home alive. From that time on, he will confine his anti-coyote campaigning to loud barking and then only if his master is right behind him. Like most other unpleasant experiences, one treatment lasts a lifetime. The dog that gets away with his life has no desire to crowd his luck. Very few dogs have the courage, or are stupid enough, to try for Lesson Two.

Coyote pups are about as unlike their sleek elders as it's possible to get. The litters generally range from four to six, although there are sometimes larger ones. The pups are nursed by the mommas for a time but once their eyes are open and they're fairly ambulatory, they are urged to experience the sights and smells at the den entrance. Their canine nature to chew things is put into full play, usually on pieces of game poppa brings in from the hunting field. These pieces the pups joyfully maul with needle-sharp baby teeth, thereby getting both the feel and the smell of fresh game.

When the pups are big enough to crowd the den, their parents keep them hidden during the day but take them along on night prowls. The adults then cripple game and let the pups finish it off, thus teaching their young the joy of sinking their tiny fangs into live meat still struggling to live. Sometimes, gophers or mice bite back, teaching the pup to kill quickly to avoid such retaliation. Their keen noses pick up many interesting odors, some of which, like the dreaded man-scent, their parents teach them to avoid.

From all the preceding, you can readily see why the coyote is known as a canny canine. Well, in view of this intelligent wariness, coyote mortality from all causes is surprisingly high.

When the pups are turned loose by their parents, they tend to forget many of the lessons they were taught. Like the young of all species, beast or human, they have to learn for themselves. Sometimes, this learning comes at the price of life itself. Some of the lessons the

adult coyotes tried to force-feed the pups, lessons mostly given at night, need some changes during daylight hours. Daylight, for instance, brings on the top activity of their most deadly enemy – man. The pups know little difference between the horses their parents approached with no concern in the dark, and the man-ridden horses which approach them during the day. They don't know that motor vehicles, which passed them harmlessly at night, can carry deadly danger during the daylight hours.

In the Southwest, the favorite method of hunting coyotes is by scouting the countryside in a four-wheel drive vehicle, such as a Jeep. Far less popular and requiring much more physical stamina, is walking them up. When going into primitive desert areas, hunters should be sure to take extra water, food, gasoline and critical auto parts. A breakdown many miles from nowhere can be most upsetting and possibly even fatal.

In other parts of the country, these crafty canines are hunted with hounds. In the more northern latitudes, hunters go out on snowshoes or in snowmobiles. But the two methods that suit the true varminter best are hunting them with calls and shooting them at long range.

The calling of coyotes, as well as many other varmint meat-eaters, has been rapidly gaining great popularity. Calling is perhaps the most productive and exciting method of taking coyotes. Several excellent calls are available, the preferred type being the rabbit-in-distress call. It's amazing to hear the heartrending sounds an expert caller can create. He will start with an agonizing shriek, cry with gasps that make you think of a human baby, and finish up with terrified squeaks that trail off into silence.

Its effectiveness is greater with coyotes than with other animals for several very good reasons: first, coyotes are now the top predators of size of any range in which they're found; second, their ability to hear is as sharp as that of any wildlife; third, their speed afoot can bring them in over considerable distances in a short period of time.

It is amazing how often coyotes will come to such calling with almost headlong abandon. They probably reason that no animal or bird that has hold of a stricken rabbit can offer much opposition or danger to them. This behavior is quite constant in such calling. The largest varmints in any given area will respond to calling most rapidly and, to a great degree, most recklessly. Obviously, the smaller critters come in more slowly because they don't cover ground as quickly. Also, they want to be sure they're not running into a larger predator of a size and nature to be of danger to them.

Of course, coyotes won't come to such calling unless the caller gets to his fixed position without drawing attention to himself. That means almost complete silence, plus an approach into the wind. Finally, the caller must keep himself in some sort of cover which breaks his outline, yet gives him a good view of the areas from which coyotes may come. Camouflaging clothing is virtually a must.

Early morning and late afternoon are when coyotes are most active. Also, these are the times of day when they can most readily be seen. Therefore, these are the best times for successful calling and hunting. A light wind helps conceal those sounds which the hunter normally makes. However, if the wind blows up around 10 miles per hour, the caller's range of coverage will be quite limited. In higher winds, the coverage becomes so limited that it is almost a waste of time to go out.

In order to cover the most area as closely as possible, it is best for two hunters to work together. Sitting nearly back to back, they can cover the entire 360 degrees of the compass. In this way, they can prevent a coyote from slinking up behind them.

Some experts feel that only 15 or 20 minutes should be spent calling from any one spot. Then you should move on a few hundred yards. Others claim it's better to call for 10 or 15 minutes, then keep calling at intervals in the same spot for half an hour before moving at least a mile away. Much depends on the area and how hard the coyotes have been hunted there. Try both ways, or variations, then decide which is best for you.

True-blue hunters prefer to stalk and shoot coyotes at long range. If this is your "bag," you must have good binoculars. A 7 x 35 or 8 x 35 will do adequately.

When choosing the gun with which to hunt this critter, it will serve you well to consider the advantages of a flat-trajectory, high velocity rifle. This animal is a surprisingly tough customer and your bullet had best strike his vitals on the first shot if you want to make sure of bagging him. Recommended loads include the larger, center-fire .22 calibers, the Winchester .270 and .284 and the Remington .280, the .30 caliber and the 7mm. These hard-hitting bullets do remarkably well. Take note that you will be doing most of your shooting on fairly open terrain and at contrasting ranges. Therefore a fitted, variable scope such as a 3x-9x will do well.

Not too uncommonly, a coyote that is thoroughly convinced that he is really on to a squealing, dying rabbit, is apt to run headlong into the concealed hunter who is using the call. To be prepared for such an occurrence, many varminters tote a scattergun as well as a rifle. Should the coyote get within thirty yards or so, the shotgun, loaded with No. 2's or larger pellets will provide the final medicine very nicely.

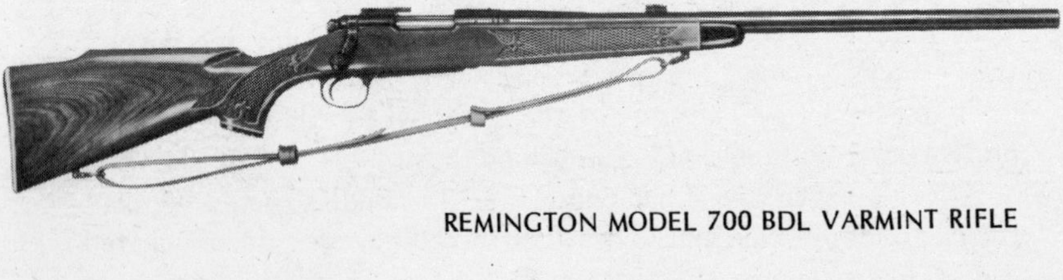

REMINGTON MODEL 700 BDL VARMINT RIFLE

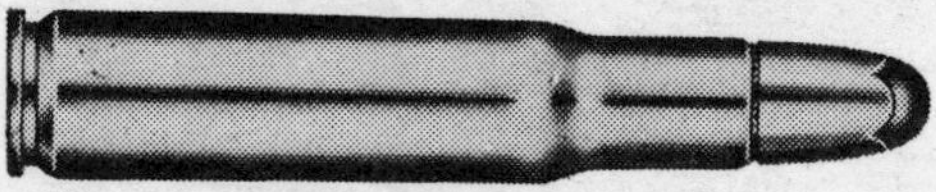

.30 REMINGTON

.270 WINCHESTER

.280 REMINGTON

7MM REMINGTON MAGNUM

It is a curious fact that once a coyote is attracted to a call, he'll most often head in a beeline, straight as an arrow, for the source of the distress signal. The only thing that will swerve him from this direct approach is the hint of something amiss. It is at this juncture that he will alter his course and turn away. At the very instant of direction change, you must squeeze off your shot. Coyotes don't hesitate to take off for parts unknown when they are alarmed by a sign or scent of danger. And when they go, they'll make a drag racer seem like a truck going uphill.

Chapter 4
The Winged Piranhas

Don't let the beauty of the magpie beguile you. Wrapped up inside that magnificent plumage is a package of feathered fury unrivaled by anything that flies. One dictionary defines *magpie* as "any of numerous birds *(especially of the genus Pica)* related to the jays." Be that as it may, this customer is closely akin to the crow in his marauding techniques, his indiscriminate decimation of other birds' nests, their eggs and fledglings alike.

However, magpies lust after bigger game and when determined, very few chosen victims can prevail against them. They are aerial assassins of the first degree. The first degree in this sense, meaning premeditated murder. Most assuredly they plan their forays. Generally they strike the newborn, defenseless young of sheep, antelope, deer, swine and yes, even cattle. It is not beyond their capabilities to slay full-grown specimens of the aforementioned, but they only prey upon the sick or injured adults.

You will be stunned by the vicious techniques employed by these birds as they systematically butcher their hapless victims. They use the mob foray system much like that of piranhas or sharks in a feeding frenzy. One typical method employed by these beautiful butchers is to peck the eyes out of a young, defenseless victim and when this is accomplished and the prey is totally unable to help itself, the magpies systematically proceed to eat it alive.

When striking at a larger, failing animal, their technique varies to the extent that they will approach their grisly job from the other end. That is, they start by tearing at the victim's rump around the base of the tail and this keeps up as they swarm in maniacal relays, until the area is completely eaten away. It is now a relatively simple matter for the killers to enter the stricken animal and satiate their hunger on its vitals.

This method is employed when they come across an animal plagued with an open sore. The same gang technique is used. Only here, nature lends the slayers a hand by causing air to rush into the gaping wound and thereby hastening the process of death. Now the murderers are free to feed at their leisure and this they do with great relish.

Some conservationists make the claim that the magpie serves man in a beneficial way by consuming great quantities of destructive insects. Forget it. They are out-and-out murderers, indiscriminate in their choice of victims and merciless in their methods. Unlike many other *so-called* killers, this is one that should be slain at every opportunity. If you see one, shoot it. That is, *if you can.*

You will recognize the magpie by the following description: The plumage on the tail, wingtips, neck and head is a brilliant black, with an iridescence that casts off glints of green when touched by sunlight; the body and upper wing surfaces are white, and the combination of dark and light form a magnificent, harlequin-like appearance that is really stunning. But as stated previously, don't be taken in by their beauty. These birds are butchers.

During the warm months of late spring and on into summer, an excellent place to seek out this winged varmint is in the meadows of high grass or in hay fields that contain goodly numbers of grasshoppers. Here is where the marauders swarm to eat their fill of the insects. You should now take advantage of the tall grass to conceal your presence as you attempt your stalk. Procede with the utmost caution because you are seeking out the wariest, most intelligent avian target on the North American continent. Nothing will tempt them to remain in the area once they've discovered your presence.

Why do we question your ability to knock down a magpie upon

MAGPIE

sight? Perhaps the following will explain our skepticism. First: The magpie is an extremely wary and intelligent bird. He never presents a simple target. Second: His size is deceptive in that he appears to be larger than he really is. This bird is mostly wings and tail, with a comparatively small body. Third: His speed in flight is very deceptive. Apparently he is flying at great speeds when in fact he is going at a fairly slow rate. Most gunners will be fooled into leading the birds by too great a distance and thereby missing many an otherwise simple shot.

A most effective method of hunting magpies is to conceal yourself in a well-hidden blind. The bait nearby your place of hiding can be an animal carcass or perhaps the inner organs of a freshly field-dressed game kill. Should there be magpies in the vicinity, you may be sure that they'll home in on the remains to begin a revelry of wild feeding.

Another method of hunting these birds is by calling. But here again, a word of caution . . . as you must remain hidden when shooting crows, so you must stay concealed once you've established your hiding place. Try your utmost not to move. If you are detected by the birds, forget trying to shoot from that spot. The hunt, for all intents and purposes, is ended. Pack up and leave the area and perhaps try someplace else out of the general vicinity.

Assuming that all has gone as it should and you have not been detected, start calling, persistently, to create an infernal racket. Magpies are extremely curious and a few might come to investigate, figuring an injured varmint will result from all the noise; or, maybe a band of crows has discovered a feast which they can share. If you should be skilled or lucky enough to shoot one, others will come to investigate. Like their crow cousins, magpies will fly to a comrade in distress.

However, unlike crows, magpies rarely gather in really large flocks, except in winter or around town dumps and slaughterhouses. Another favorite gathering place is at abandoned farms and ranches.

Naturally, the best way to shoot as many of these noisy critters as possible is to locate their roosting place. They are usually found in a thick grove of willows bordering a stream. The birds generally arrive at their roost well toward dark. So, you have to arrive early in the afternoon, set up your blind and hide in the roosting area. It's best to be outfitted in camouflage clothing with a head net and wait, with as little movement as possible. If you do all that, you'll get in some hot shooting before you frighten away the rest of the flock. Then forget all about that particular roosting spot. After being shot at, the surviving magpies will find a new roost, so don't waste your time returning to the same place the next day.

Unlike crows, magpies usually fly in quite low, often slipping in among the branches of scrubby trees and shrubs. If you are calling from a dry wash, you must be totally on the alert every moment. The showy birds may zoom over the edge of the wash barely a yard off the ground and within 15 yards of your position. For this type of shooting, shot sizes from No. 7½ to No. 9 are effective; they don't leave magpie-size holes in the patterns at any reasonable range. A skeet load of No. 9 shot is probably the most effective. The shotgun itself should be a lightweight model, capable of a fast mount and an easy swing, bored from modified to full choke.

Another method of getting magpies which has gained some popularity is trapping. These birds can be trapped quite easily in a wire-mesh trap with a ladderlike entrance. Almost any kind of food, like sliced-up jackrabbit carcass, meat trimmings acquired from a friendly butcher, any available carrion, or even grain will serve nicely as bait. If you really want a quantity catch, the ladderlike entrance should be taken away for some days and the bait placed in the trap twice a day . . . after dark and at midday. In this manner, the trap is ready for the birds during their normal feeding times of shortly after dawn and again at mid-afternoon. When the wild birds get used to having food regularly available to them, and on schedule, they'll often descend on the trap in great numbers, piling in through the ladderlike entrance with abandon. Good-sized catches can be made in just a few settings.

And don't worry about using old, weathered boards in your trap construction. Magpies won't shy away from traps made of new lumber and wire, just so long as they are placed a goodly distance away from any human use and activity . . . and there's plenty of bait.

Invariably, several small traps are more successful than one large one. They are easier to build, are more portable, cover more sites and can be tended with very little extra expenditure of time, energy and cost.

Traps that can't be visited too often require a somewhat different method of baiting. You see, when confined in a trap, the birds will eat all the edible bait. Then, when free-flying birds come near, there's nothing to lure them into the trap. Therefore, such traps should also be baited with some eye-appealing but inedible bait. For this purpose, you can use fresh beef bones, egg shells, colored China eggs, chunks of fur, hide, or feathers.

Of course, you should never do any shooting near domestic livestock or poultry without first getting permission from the owner. Livestock can be frightened into stampeding into fences or be otherwise injured. You should establish your blinds far enough away from these domestic animals so that the sound of gunfire will be muted to an unfrightening degree.

The nesting areas of magpies are easily located. They build

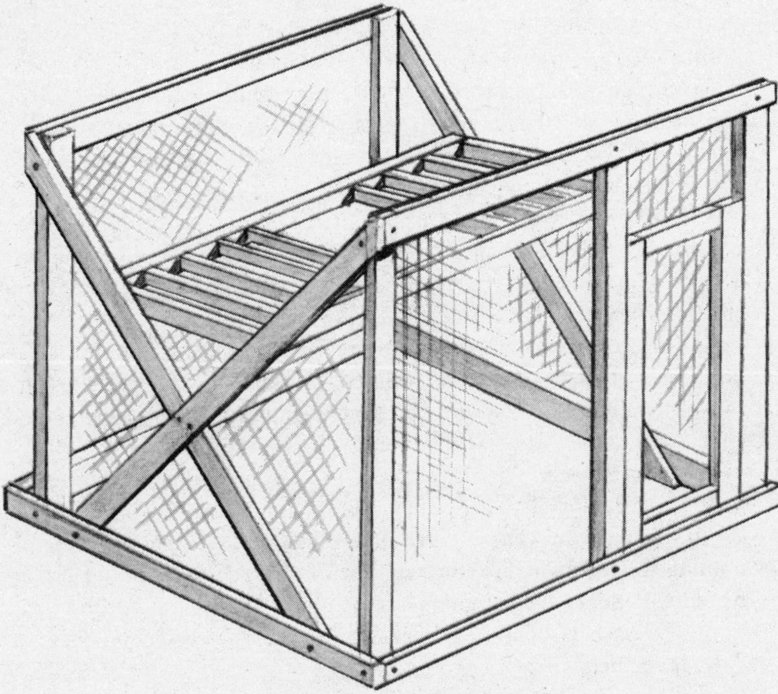

TRAP FOR MAGPIES

MAGPIE NEST

massive structures, frequently 18" wide x 24" high. They are usually six or more feet off the ground and resemble a disorderly cluster of twigs, as though the birds simply dropped the building material into the crotch of a tree as they flew by. The living space is in the center of the nest and the entrance is at the side.

Everytime you see a group of these nests in a growth of trees or brush, you know you're in for some fine pass shooting. As the families (two adults and, as a rule, four young) return to their nests after a day of devastation, they provide a great gunning treat. If magpies are numerous in your area, there may be upwards of a 100 of these polka-dotted pests crossing your sights in an evening.

No shooter who really wants to test his skill with either rifle or shotgun can afford to pass up a match with a magpie.

The guns and ammunition selected for use in magpie hunting are the same as those used in hunting crows. However, a greater shooting skill is required for any hunter to be successful against magpies. There aren't many shooters who can boast of having filled their bag with these winged piranhas.

Chapter 5
Fang and Beak

There are many different forms of snakes on the North American continent, both poisonous and harmless. Of course, for the protection of both humans and livestock, the poisonous types are either caught alive or destroyed wherever and whenever they are found. There is a market of sorts for trapped poisonous snakes among zoos, carnivals, reptile gardens and biological laboratories. The first-named three buy these catches for exhibition purposes; the laboratories take the venom from the snakes which is then used in the production of different types of serums and in other experimental work.

Most reptiles hibernate during the cold winter months in the northern latitudes. Turtles, which are biologically classified as reptiles, seek the soft mud they find at the bottom of streams. There they dig in and bed down until warm weather returns. Snakes, however, have no way to dig in anywhere. So they seek out cracks in the ground, holes, or any other opening in the earth that will take them below the normal frost line. Where such shelters are scarce, you may not find any snakes at all for miles around. But in areas that snakes can reach by travelling from their dens during the first half of summer, there may likely be a heavy reptile population. During the latter part of summer, with cold weather approaching, these snakes start their trek back to the den. If any misjudge the distance or overestimate their ability to travel quickly, they may get caught by early snows or frost . . . and die before getting home.

One of the most graphic examples of "Brotherhood-in-Action" can be found in a large hibernating den of snakes. There you will find many species intertwined in a mass, much like worms in a fisherman's baitbox. There, harmless snakes like the garter and bull integrate with the poisonous snakes like the rattlers, all wrapped around each other for the common warmth and survival of all.

The entrances to these dens are often quite small and may have numerous openings. In the spring, snakes come out on a temporary basis, because of the uncertainty of the weather. They will lie around the den entrance, basking in the new warmth of the sun; but ready to go back underground at the first sign of a reversal in weather. It is this in-again, out-again traffic that polishes the den entrances in such a characteristic manner that a knowing snake hunter can spot them quite easily.

Trapping is, by far, the most effective manner in which to eliminate the greatest number of snakes in the shortest possible time . . . with the least expenditure of time, energy and money. The following will illustrate the operation of one particular trapper who specialized in catching rattlesnakes.

Many dens he found himself and others he would find by following the leads given him by others who had noticed large populations of rattlers in a given area.

This trapper drove a pickup truck which carried a snake-tight box, for transporting his catches, and three other pieces of equipment. These were a wooden-handled steel hook for dragging the buzz-tails out of crevices and for picking them up off the ground; another steel tool with a forceps-like contraption at one end for grabbing snakes that were trying to get back in their holes; and a stout bag in which his catches could be carried to the truck.

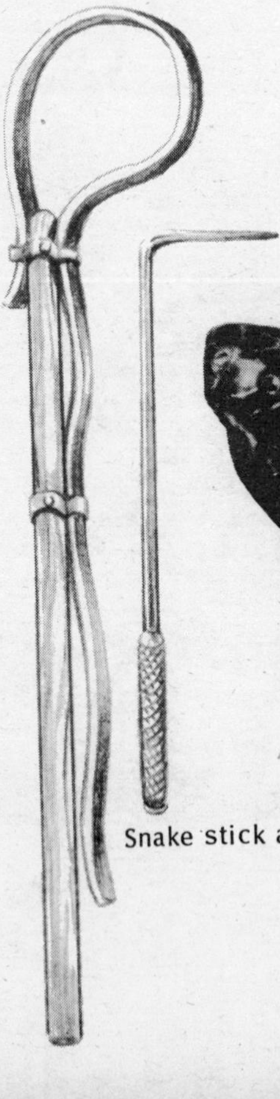

Snake collecting bag

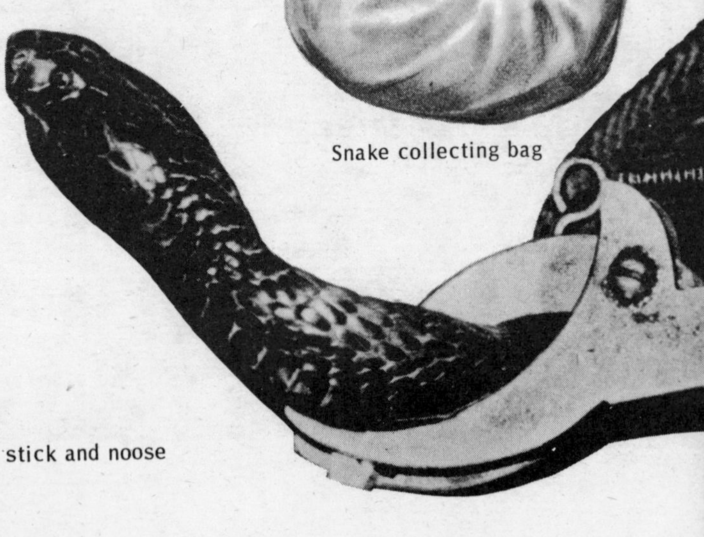

Snake stick and noose

One of the most important things you must have when hunting and trapping poisonous snakes is a very high degree of respect for even the smallest of the species. Therefore, this trapper always protected his legs by wrapping them tightly and thickly with burlap or other coarse, thick cloth. Over the cloth he would put on a pair of hip waders. This provided protection when he had to wade in among snakes at their den entrances to rake them away from the underground safety they looked for at his approach. By never hand-handling these reptiles, for the purpose of showing off, and by taking every precaution possible, he spent a lifetime of rattlesnake trapping without ever having been bitten.

His traps were simple boxlike frames of wood with an overlay of fine-mesh wire. The opening in the bottom of the box was overlaid by a

rubberized flap, fastened to the box at only one end. Snakes coming out of their den for some sun would crawl under the flap to get into the box. Then the flap would fall back into place and there was no way the snake could return to the safety of his den.

Was this trapper successful in his endeavors? Well, in a career spanning many years, he located hundreds of dens and removed tens of thousands of the rattlers . . . each year.

There is a relatively narrow range of temperatures during which snakes, especially rattlers, are active. This range is around 70 degrees at the cold end and approximately 85 degrees at the hot end. When the temperature goes below their cold-tolerance level, these reptiles become quite sluggish. Therefore, they seek shelter underground; first, to keep warm and secondly, for protection against natural enemies while they can't move quickly enough to protect themselves.

Temperatures above their heat-tolerance level will also drive them to seek shelter, especially from the direct rays of the sun. They simply cannot tolerate extreme heat, especially that of the direct sun and the reflected heat from dry sand and rocky soils. If, for some reason, a rattler can't get out of this intolerable area, it can easily wind up being "baked."

This helps explain why rattlers are out of their dens during daylight hours in spring and autumn but stay in their dens during the day and don't come out until sundown in summer. With this knowledge, farmers and ranchers can easily find and destroy rattlers who use their buildings as temporary shelters. Just look for them during daylight hours in spring and autumn. In summer, the best time to look for them is shortly before dark or early in the morning, when they're either just emerging from or going back to their shelters. One very important piece of advice: Keep small children indoors during the hours when these killers are apt to be out of their shelters and most active.

Prairie rattlesnakes usually are born toward the end of August. They shed their skins about ten days after birth and go out in search of food immediately thereafter. They usually start on young mice but can kill and swallow mature mice at this time. The following spring, they start to prey on the young of small birds and gophers.

For those hunters who have no interest in capturing live snakes nor in saving the carcass for skinning, any handgun, rifle, or shotgun will do the job of killing these dangerous specimens of the varmint kingdom. In days gone by, a most popular weapon was a handgun loaded with comparatively fine shot so that sharp aim and accuracy weren't necessary to score a kill. Also, in tight spots where a fast and deadly shot was called for, such loadings were most efficient.

However, the U. S. Department of Alcohol and Tobacco Taxation, which has jurisdiction over the legality of firearms, ruled these shot-loaded handguns illegal, classifying them as sawed-off shotguns. Therefore, effective as they may be, don't use them. If you want to shoot snakes with a handgun, you must use standard bullets.

Now, on to another member of the reptilian clan . . . the turtle.

Of the many species of turtles, only two are of economic importance and are, quite infrequently, harmful to mankind. The first of these, and the one we're going to concentrate on here, is the common snapping turtle, known as the snapper. This member of the reptile family is found chiefly in the northern half of the United States and to some extent in southern Canada. The other turtle which is of some concern because of its feeding habits and its relationship to mankind is the much larger alligator snapper of the South. Unless we use the word "alligator," all further references to "snapper" will be regarding the common snapper of the North.

A recluse by nature, snapping turtles prefer to remain hidden from view. Being extremely cautious, they avoid contact with strangers whenever possible. This is true even in the watery world in which they dwell among myriads of their own kind.

They remain quite close to their aquatic homes, seldom requiring more than a few steps to enable them to dive to safety into the protective depths. Generally speaking, they are considered rather benign creatures. But beware when you've got one cornered out of his watery element. At this juncture he becomes a very mean foe indeed. His degree of belligerency is in direct ratio to the length of time he is prevented from returning to the water. The longer the time, the meaner he becomes.

This turtle is endowed with an awesome weapon. It is in the form of a great, shearing beak that can sever any protruding appendage with an efficiency that will stun you. During the time the turtle is enraged or feels endangered, it goes into an act worthy of an Academy Award. At this moment, the reptile huffs and puffs and makes sinister, hissing sounds, saying to all the world, "Watch out for me! I'm rough and ready to fight." Should the beast be attacked, he will defend himself in a frightening manner by striking out at his tormentor with the speed of a bullet, using his horny, knife-edged beak. When open, this weapon exposes a pulsating white maw.

The snapper strikes in an upward direction, sometimes supplementing its darting neck with a forward lunge of its body. The upward move is probably due to the fact that the snapper's eyes are set on top of its head, no more than an inch behind its nostrils.

The snapper's front feet are quite strongly and sharply clawed. The hind feet are also clawed, but these are shorter and much more dulled. The tail makes one think that the snapper is a descendant of the dinosaur in that it is made up of knobby humps.

But much in the manner inherent to most turtles, the snapper uses its rock-hard shell as its prime means of protection. Immediately upon feeling set upon, the turtle retracts all exposed portions of his anatomy into the secure confines of his armor-like shell. Nevertheless, he will not demur for an instant to thrust out with that fearsome beak should he feel endangered.

When teased by a stick, it will snap at it and hang on for some seconds, especially if the stick is moved around. It may even extend its front feet to aid in its resistance to being dragged. But it will soon let go of any such inanimate object. However, if it is offered a meat target, it will hang on to it as though its very life depended on not letting go. There seems to be an instinctive feeling that it is inflicting pain and suffering on its enemy. Then those frontal claws really come into play, holding down any natural prey and placing it so that the beak can tear off mouthfuls of food. Those same claws are also most helpful in climbing slippery logs, rocks or mud banks.

It is a reflex, protective action that prompts the snapper to retract its head into the sheltering confines of its shell immediately upon grasping hold of a toe, finger or any other part of its foe. It is quite possible that this defensive gesture is stimulated by an inherited signal to protect its neck from being severed by its enemy. The one thing to remember should you ever be unfortunate enough to be caught in the predicament of having an appendage grasped by a snapper's jaws is . . . don't try to pull yourself loose, because it is in the nature of the beast to resist any attempt at extracting the member in direct ratio with the effort used to free it. Also its neck is strong enough to withstand the pull that would be required to release the entrapped part. It is virtually impossible to get free without doing severe damage to yourself. Torn flesh, crushed bones, lacerations and severe bleeding will most certainly be the result.

The question then arises, how best to free yourself? Well, there are two answers. The first is to shoot the snapper through his head, destroying the brain. It is hardly necessary to warn you that extreme caution should be taken to avoid damage to the entrapped appendage. This can come about by the shattering of the small-caliber bullet, allowing some fragments to imbed themselves in your flesh. Injury can also be caused from powder burns by too close proximity to the gun muzzle when firing.

It is quite possible that no firearm is available. What then? Well, find a stick, stem, stiff weed, small branch or perhaps a pen or pencil

and poke the weapon into the animal's nostril or eye. The shock of this will usually cause the turtle to open his mouth and thereby allow you to release yourself.

The least dangerous method of handling a snapper is by grasping the tail and holding the beast at a distance great enough to prevent him from reaching your body or limb with those frightful jaws.

It is quite possible to kill a snapping turtle with a shot through its body but a head shot is a much more efficient way of slaying the reptile. When shot through the body the reflex actions of the turtle will almost always permit the animal to reach the water, which as mentioned earlier is always in close proximity. Once beneath the surface, retrieval can prove difficult indeed. This is no time for the hunter to fumble around, feeling for the wounded beast because it is likely that in so doing, he'll wind up with one or more fingers in his intended victim's vise-like jaws.

When out of sight, it is impossible to be certain that the turtle is dead. Having been shot in the body and not the head, in all probability the dangerous beak is undamaged and can wreak havoc upon a groping hand that comes too close . . . thus, a quite obvious reason for preferring a head shot. Another salutary effect of such a shot is that it often serves to anchor the beast in place by stunning him, thereby enabling you to grab him by the tail, thus preventing him from retreating to the water.

For close shooting, a .22 pistol will do nicely. For shots further out, a .22 scope-sighted rifle is ideal.

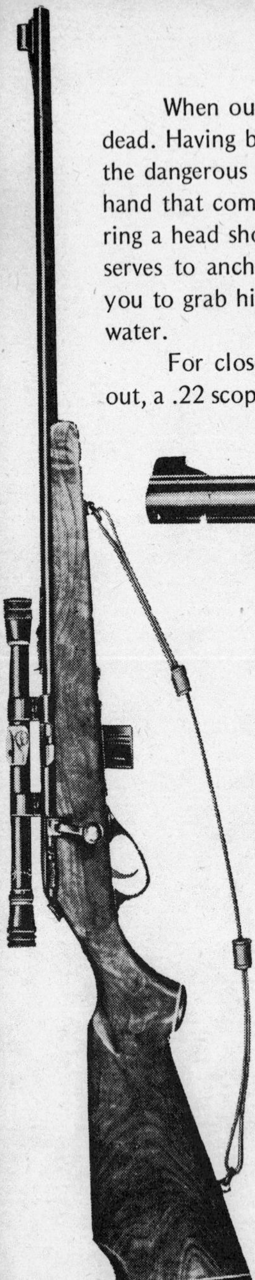

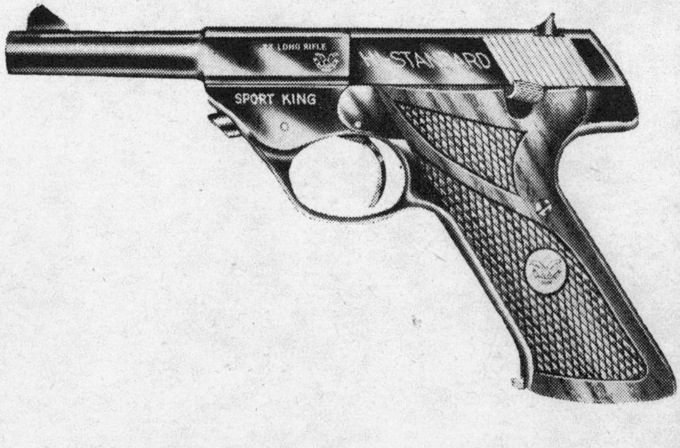

There are quite a number of men who make their living by trapping turtles, which they sell to soup manufacturers. Incidentally, if you've never tasted snapper soup, give yourself a treat some day soon.

One of the best times to live-trap snappers is when they are hibernating. They generally hibernate in the soft bottoms of lakes, streams and swamps, usually under several feet of water. Where ideal hibernating conditions are in short supply, there may be scores of snappers hibernating in stacked piles in one area. Catches in such spots sometimes reach fantastic levels.

TRAP FOR SNAPPING TURTLE

Snappers much prefer fresh food to carrion. So bait your traps with fresh frozen fish, cut up into chunks. Then put the chunks into fine-mesh wire bags. This will lure the snappers into your trap but will prevent them from eating the bait. In this manner, the bait will remain intact to attract still more snappers. The traps should be placed upstream in flowing water or upwind of the snappers in still water. In either way, the bait scent is carried to the snapper. Of course, the entrance to the trap should be facing the approaching turtle.

Many tales have been told about the great age achieved by snapping turtles. In most instances they are not exaggerations. Turtles are remarkably long-lived. There is a sound reason for their longevity, in that their life-style consists of feeding not too often and a regular cycle of winter hibernation. These factors, coupled with an extremely low metabolic rate and no natural enemies except man, make it easy to see how ages of over 100 years are possible.

These hulking beasts are in no way susceptible to a natural decimation of their numbers. Relatively speaking: they are not harmful to mankind but do prey primarily on aquatic wildlife, which is rapidly dwindling in proportion to the needs of sportsmen. The present imbalance between supply and demand calls for adjustment to fill the ever-growing needs of the outdoor sportsman. Therefore, the varminter helps to restore a balance.

Chapter 6
The Varmint Villager

Those vast, open stretches of the American Plains, known as the Prairies, are the home of a busy rodent construction engineer. This critter ranks high on the list as a favorite varmint target. It is most commonly called a "prairie dog," but it is in no shape, manner or form even closely akin to a dog; nor is it a member of the marmot family as some folks believe. Instead it is one of the ground squirrel clan. This rather small animal has the appearance of a diminutive Eastern groundhog. It is a company-loving, extremely fruitful creature.

In the early days of our nation, the "cities" or "towns" constructed and tenanted by these "dogs" were unbelievable in size. Many such settlements encompassed several hundred square miles and harbored millions of rodent residents. Currently, however, the population has dwindled to a scant reminder of the olden days. They posed such a genuine threat to the burgeoning agricultural community that they were very nearly wiped out by poisoning. Those colonies that still remain are scattered. In spite of their diminished numbers, they are still a menace to crop-producing areas and grazing lands. It is for this reason that ranchers and farmers welcome the varmint hunter on their property. Population control of the prairie dogs is essential.

The typical prairie dog town consists of a group of dens burrowed into the ground, straight down, and then interconnected by tunnelling. The usual den consists of a hard-packed, cone-shaped entrance which has two specific purposes: first, it allows quick entrance in an emergency; secondly, it acts as a dam against rising waters caused by occasional cloudbursts and/or rapid melting of winter snows. A doggie who suddenly finds himself in danger can simply fling himself into the conical entrance, release all holds and toboggan several feet below ground level. In this way, it can easily avoid surface attacks by hawks,

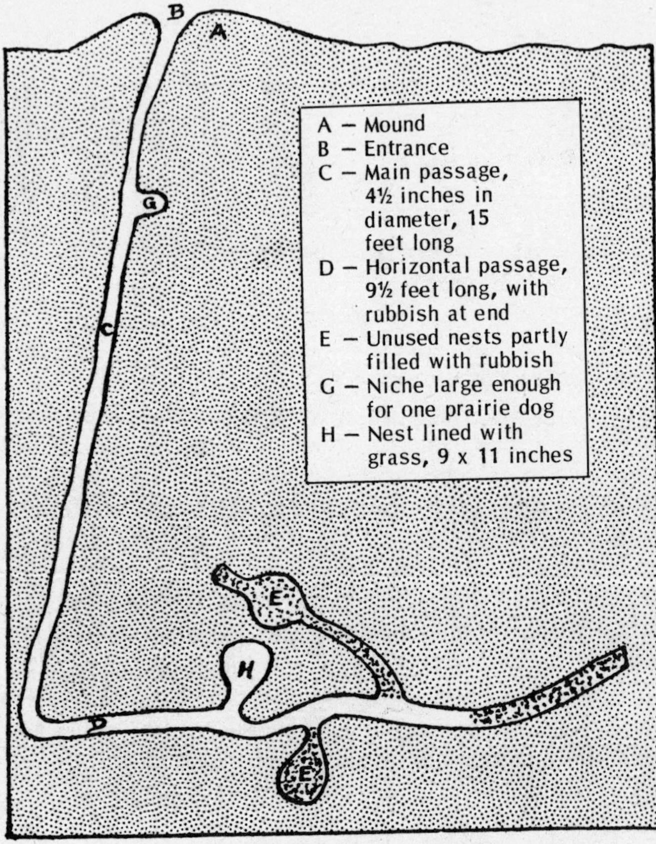

PRAIRIE DOG BURROW

eagles, coyotes, badgers, or any other meat-eaters that relish its flesh.

The den, after its initial plunge into the earth, interconnects with many other dens, thus furnishing a great many escape tunnels, each with its own exit to the surface. Each of these tunnels can be plugged with dirt to keep out water that might otherwise drown its occupants, or to prevent the passage of such underground enemies as rattlesnakes and weasels.

There are two different species of prairie dogs. The white-tailed seem to prefer the rangeland of high elevation, oftentimes being found in meadows at 8,000 to 10,000 feet. The black-tailed, on the other hand, usually establish their towns around 3,000 to 4,000 feet above sea level. Both forms are very clannish. As long as their locale offers plenty of food, they'll devote much of their time to digging and enlarging their network of dens.

These dog towns require a good deal of food. The well-padded outlines of these stocky rodents are no accident. These critters forage endlessly during the daylight hours. About the only time they're not out eating up pasture land is when sharp rains are falling or during a period of extreme heat when the dogs sleep away the broiling hours.

Like many other plains creatures, they are well adapted to arid conditions. They need almost no water, inasmuch as they own the ability to find enough water in their food supply to support their bodily functions. They have been observed emerging from their dens after a strong rainstorm, which had followed a period of extreme drought. Not a one of them even attempted to drink any of the standing water. Obviously, they relied on this moisture being absorbed into plant foods. Therefore, they get both food and drink in the same meal.

Undoubtedly, the major reason that prairie dogs have survived in areas where larger and swifter animals have steadily declined in population, is that these critters seldom offer themselves as easy rifle targets. Had this not been the case, they would surely have been exterminated long ago since they live in a section of the nation where great skill with a rifle is a common commodity. Among the varmint hunting fraternity, the dogs are considered as formidable adversaries and are thought to be "tougher nuts to crack" than most other small game.

The gunners figure they're shooting at par if they score one "dog" for every three shots. If half of their shots produce kills, they're having a sensational score. Only when a hunter is fortunate enough to come upon a "virgin" village, one that hasn't been shot over previously, can he score as high as 75 percent kills.

If we were asked to describe the prairie dog in terms of his contour as a target, the most appropriate reply would be to state that he is three targets stacked one upon the other. Starting at the top you are presented with a lemon-shaped head firmly positioned on a small but powerful neck. Immediately beneath the head is the second vital zone, the chest. This area is a bit larger than the head, but not by much. Finally, at the bottom of the pile are the pot-belly and hindquarters. When sitting upright, the "dog" presents you with these areas much in

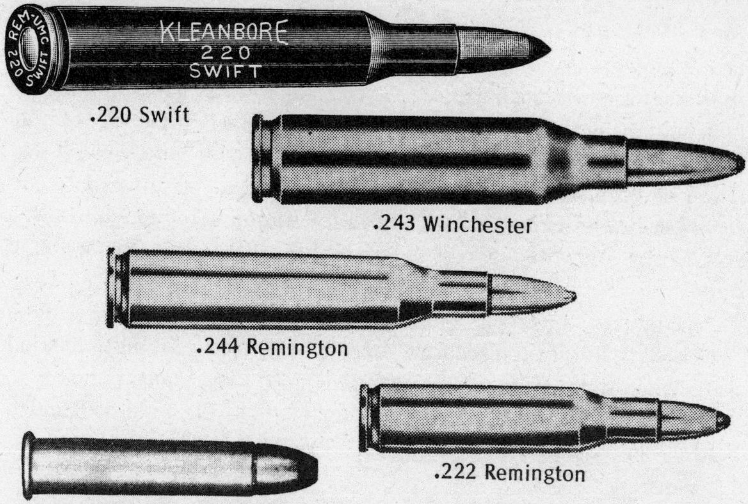

.220 Swift

.243 Winchester

.244 Remington

.222 Remington

.22 Winchester magnum

CARTRIDGES FOR PRAIRIE DOGS

the same manner as three bullseyes in vertical order. The animal is unusually muscular and his running gait is best described as a sinewy, released-bow motion.

Despite his apparent awkwardness, the prairie dog possesses an immense vitality and clings to life tenaciously. Therefore, it must be hit in one of the vital zones cleanly and with enough power to kill instantly. Generally speaking, if a .22 Long Rifle or .22 WMR is used, the best shot is one that will penetrate the entire body, clearing a path from one end through to the other, or severing the spinal column. If you wish to be certain of a clean kill every time a hit is scored, the following cartridges are recommended: the Remington .222, .244, .220 Swift or 6mm twins; or the Winchester .243. Even with these more powerful loads, accuracy is required; therefore a rifle must possess an extremely precise barrel, one that can maintain dispersion of the bullets to approximately one-minute-of-angle at all credible distances.

If a dog town hasn't been too heavily hunted, and the pups are not too wary, extreme range shooting is not necessary. In this situation, the .222 is preferred above the other calibers mentioned. It's not that this bullet is more capable of scoring clean kills. After a hunter has fired off about 50 shots with any of the others mentioned, his ability to hold the rifle steady begins to suffer. But the .222 has such little recoil that it can be fired steadily all day with no more ill effects than those suffered because of eyestrain, brought on by squinting too long through a scope sight. Also, its report is so insignificant that it isn't frightening to dogs.

However, for targets more than 150 yards away, the .222 and the .220 bullets are not too accurate because of their susceptibility to wind drift. When shooting in windy surroundings at longer ranges, the 6mm twins should be used. These heavier bullets fight off wind drift much better than the others.

DOG COLONY

Most states permit the use of motor vehicles as shooting stands when hunting prairie dogs. This saves the hunter a lot of labor and discomfort in lugging his gear from one shooting spot to the next. It also allows him to avoid contact with dust, rocks, cactus and other arid land incidentals. Most important, the hunter need not be afoot out in the searing sun. Also, there are more frequent targets offered because these animals are far less frightened by a motor vehicle than they are by men on foot. Another advantage is that you can shoot at better, overlooking angles.

If there is one difficulty in this type of shooting, it is that too few hunters can comfortably participate from any one vehicle. If two or more hunters try to get shots off at the same time, the muzzle blasts can be quite hard on the ears. But this difficulty is easily overcome. Simply use the rotation system of shooting. This means that one hunter starts the shoot and continues to shoot as long as he makes consecutive kills. When he misses, the next shooter in the order of rotation takes over and continues until he misses, and so forth.

When hunting these rodents, your rifle should be zeroed at around 150 yards. You see, if you're shooting over any previously gunned village, you'll get few shots closer than that. And if the village has been shot down to where the population is but a fraction of what it used to be, most of your shots will be at from 200 to 300 yards.

To be a really successful prairie dog shooter, you must be an excellent judge of distance, with a good knowledge of the trajectory of your bullets at any given range. Also, you must be able to determine wind drift. Otherwise, you will be little more than an average marksman. And, the average marksman can consider himself lucky if he averages 20 percent hits, that is one for every five bullets fired.

Along with the proper rifle, the correct cartridges and your accumulated knowledge, you need a good telescopic sight affixed to your rifle so you can properly see your target. Two of the finest of modern-day scopes are the Bausch & Lomb Balvar 8 on Kuharsky

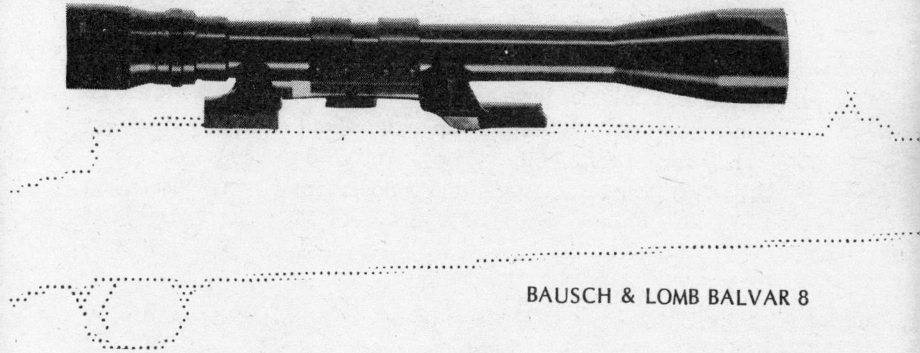

BAUSCH & LOMB BALVAR 8

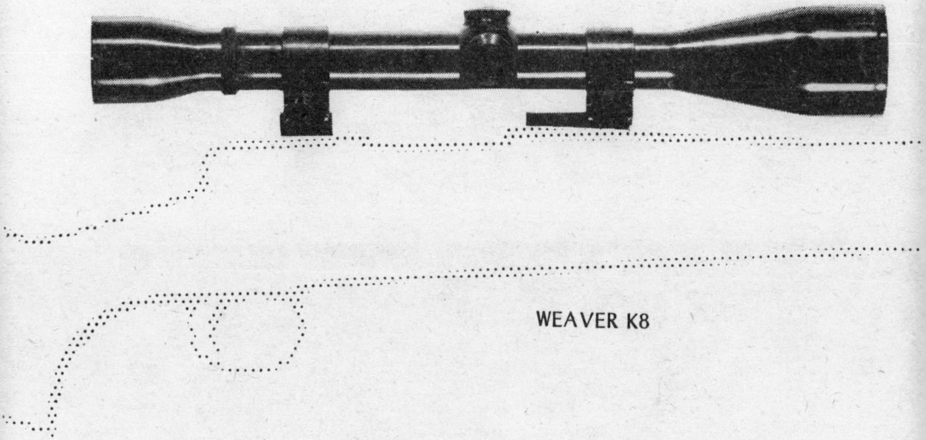

WEAVER K8

mounts and the Weaver K8 on Weaver mounts. Both of these are of the variable type. That is, they can be set at any range of magnification from 2-power up to a maximum of 8-power. Translated into English, this means that a 2-power scope setting will double the size of the target as seen by the naked eye while reducing in half the actual distance between you and the target.

Chapter 7
The Sly Ones

There are many wild stories told about the crafty intelligence of foxes, especially the red fox. So many stories, in fact, that the saying, "He's crafty as a fox" has come into common usage when referring to someone who is really clever in his ways, whether they be in business or personal endeavors. Actually, many of the tales about the slyness of these varmints would be unbelievable, except that they have been positively verified as true. Today, there is no wild creature considered more clever except the wolf and the coyote.

To illustrate how sly a fox can be, there is on record the verified story of a man who came upon a fox in his hen house. The fox, unable to escape, promptly rolled over on its back, with its legs extended straight up in the air, pretending to be dead. The farmer was completely taken in by this act. He lifted the fox up from the ground and carried it outside. The crafty critter remained stiff, as if possessed by rigor mortis. However, as soon as the farmer deposited his burden on the grass outside the hen house, the fox bounded to its feet and really "scratched gravel," the dumbfounded farmer being able to do no more than watch his "dead" fox make a safe getaway. Animals, human or beastly, just don't come much smarter than that.

There are two major species of fox, the red and the gray. These two inhabit the entire United States and Canada, covering the area much like a blanket. Therefore, no matter in what section you may do your hunting, you're bound to find foxes. In most states, the hunting season starts in November. But, it's really during the first three months of the year that you'll find most of your targets of either species of fox. These wily animals have to a great extent resisted the intrusion of civilization and get along in the suburbs almost as well as in the wilder, uninhabited regions.

A singular difference between the gray and the red is in their preference for varied terrain. It is in the nature of the gray to seek the dense underbrush and thickets of the deep woodlands, while the red seems more comfortable in open farmland and rolling countryside. The red is also fond of deserted, old farms.

RED FOX COUNTRY

GRAY FOX

It used to be that the gray fox was mostly a southland animal. However, over the years he has extended his range northward, right up to the Canadian border. His pelage is quite attractive and also serves to camouflage him most efficiently. Around his face is a rust-red ruff that contrasts with the balance of his coat which is a stylish salt-and-pepper gray. There is a rather dark black strip running the length of his back from the tip of his tail up to his head. As indicated previously, the gray fox prefers dense thickets, heavily wooded tracts, swampy marshlands and generally overgrown areas that will afford him ready cover from danger. Since he is not endowed with great speed or endurance, it is his

habit to go to ground or climb a tree when pursued. Yes, I said climb a tree! The gray fox is perfectly capable of doing that.

The red fox's coat color ranges from rust-red to various shades of mid-yellow. He has lambent yellow eyes. They are strikingly oriental in their almond shape. All four feet are stockinged in black and the lushly furred tail is crowned with a pure white tip. This cousin to the gray is the more common of the two, his range extending all the way from the

Arctic Circle in the north to the Gulf states in the south. Originally a Northerner, his expansion southward was greatly induced by Southern sportsmen. These gentlemen-hunters transported a goodly number of the reds so they could have faster, hardier game for their hounds than the local grays.

As noted earlier, foxes have long had the reputation of being about the shrewdest of wildlife. And they have well earned this distinction. They are small enough to hide almost unseen right under the noses of hunters; they're sly enough to make successful raids on noisy chicken coops; they're agile enough to catch many a rabbit and game bird; and they're intelligent enough to stay out of areas of high human population.

There have been stories circulated about that foxes are difficult to trap. Well, the truth of the matter is that where both coyotes and foxes are in roughly equal number, any somewhat experienced trapper will catch himself about ten times as many foxes as he will coyotes. Though proven an exceptionally sly critter, he still does not hold a candle to the coyote. One of his problems is that he is generally much too curious for his own good. He also has some rigidly fixed habits that a good trapper or hunter can use to advantage against him. It has long been proven that a good coyote hunter can turn to foxes with great success but a good fox hunter does not find it so easy turning to coyotes.

Good coyote territory is rarely occupied by foxes. The coyotes are much larger, a good deal speedier, and know that foxes are competing with them for the same food. And there's no way they'll abide that situation. There may be times when one of the little wolves will invade a good fox area, and he will thrive there. But the reverse is seldom recorded. Probably the best reason why the two species rarely intermingle is that coyotes will simply kill foxes out in open country areas where greater speed really counts.

Most foxes are no bigger than a medium-sized dog. Their weight will range from eight to twelve pounds, which isn't much more than a well-developed tomcat. However, because of his exceedingly thick fur and large, brushlike tail, he gives a deceptively large appearance.

His small size probably accounts for his great liking for heights—the top of haystacks, tree stumps, etc. These raised elevations permit him to see farther than he would be able to do otherwise. When in dense grass or in grain fields, these critters will often stand up on their hind legs, much like a begging domestic dog, so as to be able to see over the natural obstruction.

The gray's fur is much more like coarse hair than the red's, and it's not nearly as thick. Also, the gray's feet are much larger than those of the red. Both of these differences make it somewhat more difficult for the gray to get along well in the northern latitudes. His thinner fur does not protect him from the cold as well and his larger feet tend to cause him some discomfort from occasional frostbite.

The reds are also a bit larger than the grays and far bolder in their relation to man. The red is speedier and a good deal more aggressive when the two meet. Hunters much prefer to hunt reds. Though they lay down very involved and devious trails which often bewilder hunters and hounds, they stay pretty much to the ground. When being trailed by hounds, a red may run up a somewhat slanted tree and then jump far off it; he may walk along fences or railroad tracks; he may take to a paved highway. He may walk across thin ice which can break under the heavier weight of hounds; he'll wade through streams, marshes, or shallow shore waters. In other words, he'll do anything and everything possible to break his trail. But if the hounds are capable of staying on his trail despite his shenanigans, he will also run through familiar passes where knowing hunters will be waiting for him.

The grays are quite catlike and furtive in style and not very clever in perplexing their pursuers. As noted, if pressed too closely by hounds, they will readily take to the trees and climb up some 15 or 20 feet seeking safety. In a situation such as this the gray simply does not have the inherent guile of the red.

When being chased, the red is totally different from his gray cousin. The red fox has a bag of trail tricks than can baffle the most experienced hunter. He will set down an erratic trail over, under, around, through, next to and on top of any and every bit of the countryside. This customer can cause you to wonder whether you're chasing one fox or a dozen red devils. He seems to be deriding your apparent inability to catch him. The most successful method of bagging him has been by the use of good trail hounds such as the Trigg, the Redbone and the Walker.

These dogs seem to have the stamina and endurance needed to maintain the constant pressure required to cause the fox to commit a blunder. They also possess the good noses required to sort out the cold-trail problems presented when running in full pursuit of a fox. It is while on the trail that a hound with a good voice proves to be of great value, for it is this wonderful baying sound that enables you to zero-in on the direction the pursuit is taking. One of the most thrilling sounds in all the outdoors is the magnificent bugling and deep-throated baying of a pack of trail-wise hounds on a torrid trail. As for firepower, a 12-gauge shotgun in either double-barrel or pump action will serve you well.

Another popular way of hunting foxes is with shotguns from light planes. During the winter months up north, when snow covers the ground, there is maximum visibility of the animals. Because the reds seek elevations as lookout points, you should always be sure to check out all haystacks that may be in the area. Foxes have been known to sit on top of the stack until the plane was almost roaring over them before they'd light out to try to find some cover.

Of course, hunting from a plane at that time of year can be very dangerous unless there's a really good, experienced pilot at the controls, especially in hilly country. There, the sun warms the south slopes of the hills but leaves the north slopes cold. The warm, sunny slopes cause the air near them to rise but the shaded north areas are dominated by downdrafts. Therefore, a light plane can be crashed into the ground should it cross from the sunny side into the shaded side while diving on a gunning run. A pilot on a plane hunt cannot afford to pay anything less than absolute attention to the job at hand . . . piloting the plane.

In the early days of plane hunting, pilots experimented with different ways of approaching a target. One of the methods used was to dive at right angles to the flight of the fox. But that gave the gunner only a split instant in which to get off a very difficult shot, at a target which was both moving forward and also twisting away, at the same time. Also, because of the angle of the dive, it was quite a dangerous method as it left the plane vulnerable to a crash in the event a downdraft caught it in mid-dive.

It was learned, after much experimenting and a goodly number of crashes, that it was better to approach the target from directly in back of it, parallel to its path of flight, and then overtake it at full throttle. This prevented the fox from getting under the plane, completely hiding it from a shot; the straight-ahead shot is a much more simple one than the cross angle; and the pilot has a much better chance to either pull up or land safely if a downdraft should catch the plane.

One thing that must be learned anew when hunting from a plane is the lead. On the ground, shooting as the animal crosses your line of vision, you lead to the front so that the critter seems to run into the shot. From the air, shooting along the same line the target is running,

you might assume you lead the same way, aiming ahead of the target. But, remember, the plane is going much faster than the fox. So the lead must be in reverse of everything you've done in other, more conventional forms of hunting. You have to actually hold behind the spot you want to hit. The speed of the plane will then cause the shot to carry forward to the point of impact. The amount of lead will, of course, vary with the speed of the plane but the aiming point, or hold point, will generally be somewhere along the critter's tail . . . near the tip of the tail if the plane is really fast, the nearer up toward the root the slower the plane.

SHOT

NUMBER	DIAM. IN INCHES	APPROX. PELLETS IN 1 OZ.
● 12	.05	2385
● 9	.08	585
● 8	.09	410
● 7½	.09½	350
● 6	.11	225
● 5	.12	170
● 4	.13	135
● 2	.15	90
● BB	.18	50

BUCKSHOT

NUMBER	DIAM. IN INCHES	APPROX. PELLETS IN 1 LB.
● 4	.24	340
● 3	.25	300
● 1	.30	175
● 0	.32	145
● 00	.33	130

With this reverse lead, shotshells loaded with No. 4 shot are preferred by most fox hunters. In fact, this is the load most used in all types of fox hunting. The pattern of this shot is carried forward into the chest and lung areas.

The hazards of light, low-flying plane hunting have, to some extent, been greatly reduced by the introduction of helicopters. These extremely maneuverable aircraft are far more flexible for this type of flying. They can take off from and land in almost any small clearing, can hover almost motionless over any target, can herd animals like no other type of flying machine, and can still fly fast enough to overtake foxes. They can go into many areas where light, conventional planes cannot be used. However, they do have one somewhat serious drawback. Their initial cost and the continuing expense of operation are quite a bit higher than for planes.

Of course, there are still many, many fox hunters who don't go for hunting from planes or helicopter or using hounds. Either they can't afford this type of sport or they enjoy hunting as a match of wits . . . theirs against the fox's. They simply wait until a fresh snow has fallen, go out and look up a fox trail, then mush along until they come up with their target.

It's best not to follow directly in the tracks of the fox's trail. Instead, parallel the trail from about 40 to 60 yards, keeping only a casual eye on the trail itself. Foxes, like most other wildlife, tend to watch their backtrail. For some strange reason, the fox doesn't think of any hunter not following in his exact tracks as a menace. He figures

that the man walking along way off to the side must be some kind of nut, out for a stroll in the snow. Just keep a sharp eye on weed and brush patches into which the animal's trail leads and you may well find yourself opposite your target, ready to take him out of this world, before he even realizes that you're not a nut but rather his passport to the great fox land beyond.

A less tiring but equally effective way to hunt fox is to use an artificial call. In fairly thick cover, a call much like the sound of a mouse squeak can be most productive. Of course, you must be sure to enter the cover undetected. The sound is easily produced by sucking on the saliva-moistened back of your hand. It's a low-volume sound, so it can only be used to cover relatively short distances. After all, an honest mouse call can't be heard at any great distance, not even by a sharp-eared fox.

Out in more open country, a more effective call is that of a dying rabbit. It's louder in tone and will be heard over a far greater distance. As with all game calling, you must observe the rules of remaining undetected as long as possible so that you don't spook the animal before he comes in close enough to be shot.

Whatever method of hunting you use, do not regard fox hunting as a one-time undertaking. Your first trip into a new area will usually be unproductive. It takes experience and time and careful observation to learn the paths that a fox habitually takes, what points he crosses. If you have the patience to learn to be good at what you're doing, the second trip, and certainly the third, will be most rewarding.

Always remember that the fox looks much bigger than he really is. There is no need to use a powerful bullet to kill one of these varmints. The .22 magnum and the .222 are enough to get the job done. And, of course, since foxes are generally found in relatively heavy cover and are usually shot at somewhat close range, a good ol' reliable shotgun is your best bet.

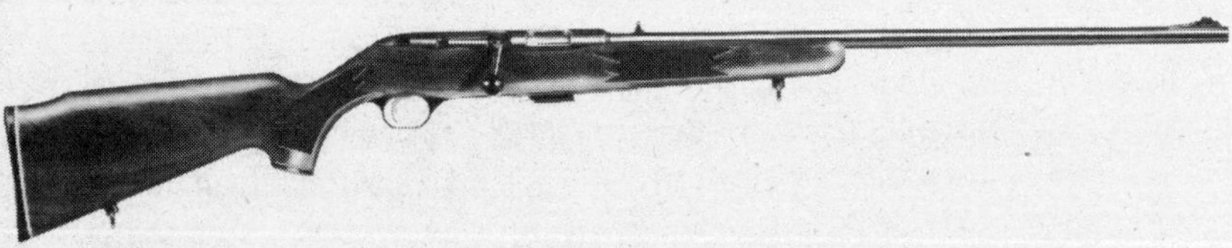

MOSSBERG MODEL 640K .22 MAGNUM BOLT-ACTION REPEATER

Just one last word of caution. Be very careful how you handle a fox, dead or alive. Under either condition, don't get bitten or tooth-scratched by one of them. And do your best to likewise protect your dogs, if you have any. You see, foxes are extremely mobile and their populations are widely distributed. Mostly because of this, these creatures are now recognized as the #1 spreaders of rabies. Another reason lies in the very nature of the animal. A domestic dog is apt to run from a coyote, frightened by its size and ugly demeanor. The dog would probably take off away from a skunk after getting one whiff. But a fox, being no larger than a medium-sized dog and having been hunted by dogs, holds no terror for the domestic animal. So, the dog jumps on the fox, bites into him, and is in turn infected by the rabid critter. The newly infected dog may easily become a danger to his owner. So be careful.

Chapter 8
Beak and Talons

Despite its relatively large size and wide range, the great horned owl is probably the least known of all the birds classified as varmints. Although its great, booming voice can be heard emanating from the deep forests of the North American continent (specifically the southern woodlands of Canada, the entire United States and well into Mexico), this creature remains a mystery to most people. Even where there are no trees, it will make its home along dry washes and on cliffs that have been eroded by eons of wind and floods, perching wherever a foothold can be found. And yet, in spite of this varied habitat and with a weight of up to six pounds, a height of two feet and a wingspread of about five feet, this amazing bird is only rarely seen. And then, only briefly.

You see, these truly large birds are really very shy. They may live quite close to human habitation but are so retiring and quiet in their hunting habits that only a watchful and keen observer ever spots one, usually as it disappears in flight.

The great horned owl is a deadly killer of precious game birds and domestic poultry, among other forms of animal life. It also has an almost insatiable appetite. The favorite dish of this varmint bird is cottontail rabbit.

This predatory bird has several features that allow it to function as a most deadly, efficient killer. Its eyes are like great illuminated orbs of blazing yellow. These amazing visual organs function in a similar fashion to the lens of a camera. They shut down to mere peep-holes in brilliant light or gape wide in the stygian darkness of moonless nights. The round head is capable of turning 180 degrees in either direction, thereby allowing a full turning and viewing radius of 360 degrees. This head is surmounted by two tufted ears that are ultrasensitive to the slightest noises at incredible distances, much in the manner of radar antennae. Added to these attributes is the ability to fly at incredible speed, enabling him to catch many game birds, including pheasants, quail, grouse and waterfowl. It is at this time that his fearsome killing tools are put to use—eight baling-hook talons of immense piercing and crushing power and a scimitar-shaped gaping beak that can tear any victim to shreds.

This scourge of sportsmen and poultry farmers possesses an amazing natural camouflage. Its plumage varies with its environmental surroundings, spanning a color spectrum of light tan-gray when in sundrenched arid areas, to a deep charcoal gray when in the gloom of a forest.

Being endowed with this wealth of natural hunting and killing weaponry, the owl is in the unique position of being able to make the best of the ebb and flow of its varied quarry. Thus the killer bird can strike when its intended victims are less wary because of a general increase in their activity.

As far as the kind of prey owls go for, they are most indiscriminate. As long as their intended victim is alive, moving, and can be grabbed by their talons, they go for it. This varmint's menu is quite varied. Among its favorite dishes are cottontail, hare, snowshoe rabbits and jackrabbits. Grouse, pheasant, and other game birds of similar or smaller size are also welcome additions to the owl's bill of fare. Domestic animals such as tame rabbits, ducks, chickens, young geese and turkeys are regular victims of the owl's grab, tear and eat attacks. These animals' wild instincts have been so blunted by years of domestication that they have become extremely easy prey for the horned assassin.

These voracious killers have been known to grab fox cubs, domestic cats, and even the animal usually safe from most prowling predators . . . the smelly skunk. You see, despite the owl's exceptionally high sense of sight and hearing, it has relatively no sense of smell.

One of the reasons why great horned owls aren't hunted more diligently than they are is their low rate of reproduction. If these deadly killers raised large crops of young, sportsmen and poultry farmers would long ago have had to make a more determined effort to kill them off.

A mated pair of owls usually nest two eggs. They generally nest in

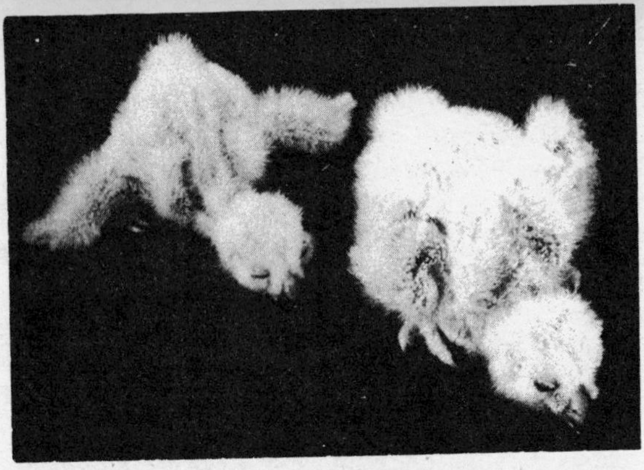

GREAT HORNED OWLETS

the previously used and abandoned nests of hawks and crows. Owls are not particularly skilled nest builders so they make do with what they find. The eggs are usually laid by early March and the female spends about a month bringing forth her brood of two. Oh yes, if you should hear a lot of owl hooting in mid-winter, it probably has nothing to do with scaring prey out into the open. It's during this period of time that these killers turn lovers.

The newly born owlets generally leave the nest by early June. Their covering of white down has been overlaid by fluffy gray-brown feathers. However, only the flight and rudder pinions of the wings and tail show a great degree of stiffness. This is because they have exercised these by clutching the shelf of the nest with their talons while flying in place byclumsily paddling into the wind.

Great horned owls are the worst predators that game farm managers have to contend with. The varmints raid the holding pens during the twilight or dawn hours and are so quick and efficient in their killing that there is virtually no warning sight or sound. One way to stop the owls from completely decimating a stock of domestic or game birds is to put up a series of poles higher than the pen posts and set them with traps. Owls like to perch on high elevations to survey the surroundings for victims before launching their killing dive-strikes. However, the best way to keep them out is to completely roof over the pens and make them owl-tight.

Due to the owl's inherent shyness and its near-perfect camouflage, this bird cannot be sought after in the traditional manner. The most advantageous way to check the overpopulation of these marauding varmints is to go out at regular intervals and examine the abandoned nesting sites of herons, hawks and crows. The nests which had been used the previous year by their original tenants will appear flattened, so that careful scrutiny through field glasses will usually reveal the presence of a female owl perching on top of the nest. You may be reasonably sure that once you've spotted a female owl incubating her eggs, her mate is usually close by—probably not farther than 75 yards from the nesting site. It is a strange fact though, that no matter at what height in the tree the nest is situated, the male owl will not perch any higher than ten feet from the ground. It would be a rare sight indeed to see him out on a high limb pinpointed against the sky making an easy target for the hunter.

An extremely difficult task for the hunter to accomplish is to approach to within good shotgun range of any nesting female. Her reflexes and natural wariness make this an almost impossible task when attempted in the ordinary manner. The one chance of succeeding is by trying your approach while the branches of the trees are being whipped by a fairly strong breeze. It is the sound of the branches striking one another that will muffle your footsteps and thereby allow you to get close enough for a shot. Oh, yes, another factor to remember is that your stalk must be made not only with complete silence but also directly into the prevailing wind. The reason is that nesting females turn into the wind to avoid having their feathers disturbed, thereby causing their body temperature to drop. This technique will assure you a better opportunity for a kill since you will be approaching from the rear. This means you will not be readily seen, heard or your scent picked up.

By this means, your close proximity will allow you to blast the nest completely. This will usually kill the female and demolish the eggs. Take note, however, the great horned owls are extremely tenacious birds and it takes a punishing load to penetrate the nest and the thick, fibrous muscles of the bird. A magnum load of No. 4 shot would not be considered too heavy.

Should you prefer the rifle to the shotgun, here are a few words of advice. If possible, note the location of the mated male and female. Usually they are in close proximity to one another during the nesting period. When spotted, take the male first and always from at least 100 yards. A shot at this distance will rarely disturb the female and she will usually remain on the incubating eggs. Should you go for the female first it is quite likely that the male will abandon the area instantly, depriving you of the opportunity to nail him.

The rifleman is faced with the need for a bullet that will penetrate the tough nesting material without fragmenting. The recommended bullet should be heavier than average and round-nosed. A lightweight, thin-jacketed round simply cannot be depended upon to do an adequate job. It is also to be noted that the male owl is quite often perched behind concealing branches and boles of small trees; hence the need for maximum penetrating power with a minimum of deflection.

MOSSBERG SLIDE-ACTION SHOTGUN, MODEL 500

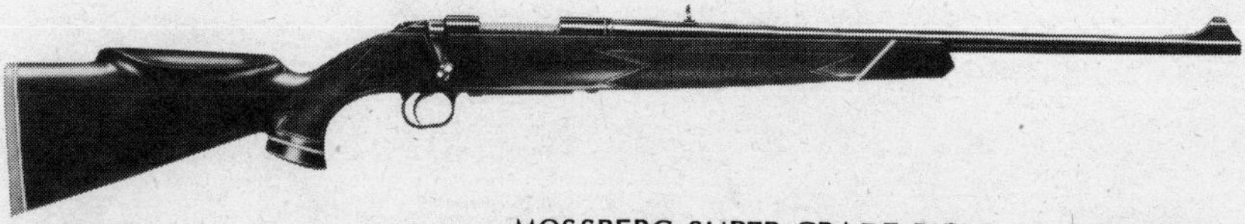

MOSSBERG SUPER GRADE RIFLE, MODEL 800D

For penetrating the tangled mass of foliage, twigs and branches that comprise the owl's domain, the really powerful varmint rifles are recommended. This category includes the following: beginning with the .222 and continuing on through the .243 and .244 twins and the .25 caliber. These carry enough weight and cohesion to go through even the hardest nesting material. They are truly potent medicine.

Chapter 9
The Wild Cats

Is there a hunter who doesn't dream of someday collecting a bobcat for his trophy room?

The bobcat is comparatively abundant, ranging over virtually the entire United States, much of southern Canada, and all of Mexico. They have adapted exceptionally well to civilization and often live in close proximity to farms and ranches. Yet, few people, even hunters, have ever seen a free-ranging bobcat in the wild. Most of those killed are as a result of being called, still-hunted, awaited on stands while being trailed by hounds, or by being treed by dogs.

These handsome cats have always had a tremendous appeal to sportsmen. And that appeal is stronger today than ever before. The extraordinary increase in the number of hunters and the resultant crowded hunting conditions have turned many a pesty varmint into eagerly sought game. As a matter of fact, bobcats—or wildcats as they are often and appropriately called—are listed as game animals in many states and can be hunted only during the open season.

The bobcat is one of the three species of varmint felines living on the North American continent. We will briefly discuss the other two further on. For the time being, we'll stay with the bobcat for the simple reason that it is the only one surviving in sufficient numbers to still be considered a challenging target in much of its range.

If ever an animal's name befitted its owner, the name "bobcat" suits this feline perfectly. It sports an abbreviated version of a tail which appears to have been "bobbed." This short appendage is creamy white or dark beige on its lower surface with a tip of black; several horizontal black stripes line the upper portion of the tail in front of the dark tip. Depending upon his environmental surroundings, the base color of his coat will vary. The specimens that dwell in open, well-lit terrain will have faded, light gray or tan pelts; while those that reside in the gloomy forests of the Pacific Northwest are more apt to wear coats of an iron-gray hue. Dappling the fur in a seemingly random pattern are a goodly number of dark spots. This subtle coloration, which acts as an efficient camouflage, coupled with the cat's nocturnal life-style, explains why the animal is so rarely seen.

Strangely enough, bobcats can be arrogantly indifferent to observation, especially if they know they've been seen. Unless a definitely hostile move is made toward them, they will rarely make any but a casual attempt to escape. They are so disdainful that one gets the impression that they just wish the nosey human would just go about his business and leave them to theirs.

When bobcats really want to be unobserved, they can disappear in places where a healthy prairie dog or cottontail would find it difficult to hide. With the aid of one of nature's finest camouflage jobs, they simply blend with and into any available cover and become almost as invisible as air.

An effective but not very sporting method of catching a bobcat is by trapping. A precautionary note is required at this time. When visiting the trap, exercise the utmost care if a bobcat has been ensnared.

For it is at this precise time that the cat turns into one of the most violent, mean-tempered coils of raging muscle in the entire animal kingdom, using every means at his disposal to hide from you—the cause of his pain. As noted previously, his camouflage allows him to blend into the slightest wisp of cover, so therefore we reiterate: Use the utmost care when approaching the cat, because he'll kill you if he can.

The fellow who could really "lick his weight in wildcats" would be quite a guy. The average fully-grown wildcat only weighs somewhere between 20 and 30 pounds. But it is nothing short of hell-on-wheels when it comes to fighting. A cornered bobcat's combination of speed, skill, and absolute ferocity is truly amazing, and sometimes borders on the fantastic. Hounds, even in packs, that can corner and successfully attack and beat a bobcat are indeed rare. These feline predators are just too much for 99 percent of all hounds. The cats can dish out more punishment per slicing stroke than even the bravest canines (except coyotes) can face up to. Like a leech, the bobcat just doesn't know when to let go once he's in a fight for survival. He won't quit until he's lost all of his proverbial nine lives.

The bobcat has much the same fighting tools as the ordinary house cat, except that they're larger and far more punishing. The predator's front paws are each edged with four exceedingly sharp cutting claws and in a fight, he uses them like a champion human boxer. Everytime he connects with his opponent, he doles out pain and draws blood. His markedly long legs give him unusual reach to go with his blinding speed. He's so fast and can keep a dog at such distance that the canine can't get his jaws into the act. A fighting-mad bobcat seems to surround his opponent. He makes a dog feel that, while he's trying to dodge one swipe of those frightful claws, he's being raked and chopped up by five others.

Nature helps keep a bobcat's claws always in superb fighting shape . . . good and sharp . . . by making them retractable, like all other cats', except the cheetah. Other animals wear down their claws against the abrasive land surfaces on which they travel. But bobcats sheathe their claws when travelling such roads. They regularly "hone" their claws against the bark of trees to remove any dulling growth and

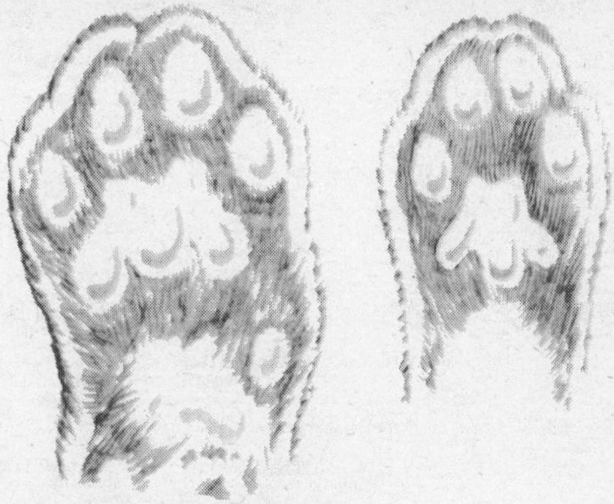

BOBCAT PADS: HIND, FRONT

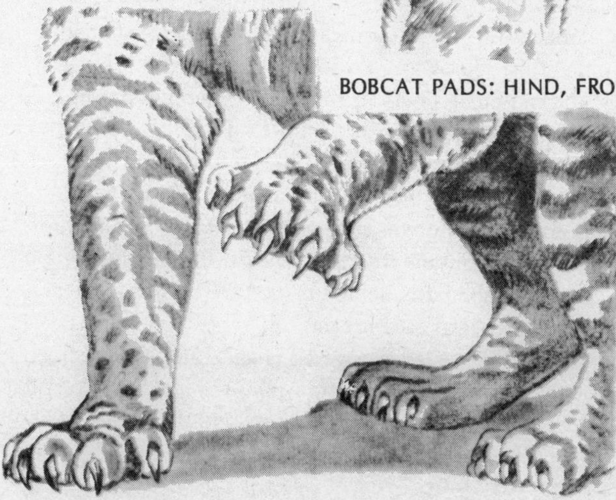

thereby save their hooking points and cutting edges for more serious work than walking.

In addition to all its other qualities, a bobcat's paws are remarkably flexible. They've been observed palming a somewhat less than cautious sparrow almost before the bird could get off the ground. The claws seem to come out and encircle the bird like the closing fingers of a man's hand. This animal's adroitness is simply fantastic.

Bobcats are sometimes pictured as fierce killers of deer and antelope as well as predators on all forms of large game. While it may be true that a large cat will sometimes go for and kill a sickly fawn or deer, especially when the cat is ravenously hungry, these are rare instances.

Their primary source of nourishment is the cottontail and other species of rabbit. But they don't overlook such other tidbits as mice, rats, gophers, squirrels, and birds. Oddly enough, there is one animal of a size which the bobcat should easily be able to handle that gives the cat problems. That is the porcupine. Because of a bobcat's stealthy approach to game and his hair-trigger pounces on his intended victim, the lowly porky, with its thousands of quills, causes great trouble. When a cat hits this target, he invariably winds up with both front paws and his face pincushioned with the needle-sharp barbed quills.

Thus, the bobcat who is too arrogant or incautious enough to leave the porcupine alone winds up in a sorry state, indeed. The quills seriously damage the muscular fibers in the face, sometimes preventing the stricken cats from eating. The inflammation that follows may reduce the cats to skin and bones and many times results in death.

The favorite method of hunting these dappled terrors is by the use of skilled cat hounds. Should you choose this technique while hunting in rugged mountain or canyon country, you had better be in good shape physically; when a bobcat is being pursued by hounds, it generally heads into the most rugged area it can find, in the hope of shaking off its pursuers. Though the distance covered is generally rather short, you'll feel as though you've just run a four-minute-mile. However, it won't be long before the hounds have treed the varmint. When this occurs, it's merely a matter of walking up to within shooting range and

finishing off the cat. A light lever-action .30-.30 woods rifle is just right for the job. You will not require a scope.

There are a number of reasons why bobcats tree ahead of hounds with such promptness. And none of them has anything to do with the comparative sizes of any given cat or dog.

It's simply against feline nature to indulge in long, exhausting runs. Their muscles aren't strong enough nor are their lungs large enough to sustain such sprints. That is why they usually creep up stealthily to within a few yards of game and then launch a furious closing attack. And if that game should escape that first attack without being crippled and make a fast run for safety, the cat will usually seek other game rather than make a chase of its first target.

Also, a bobcat which has shortly before killed game and gorged himself, will very rarely run more than a few yards before treeing. You see, unlike coyotes, bobcats don't possess the ability to regurgitate.

Therefore, when pursued, that load of meat crowds in on their already small lungs and tires them quickly.

Finally, like all felines, the bobcat just doesn't like a raucous noise in close proximity. A barking dog can quickly tree a wildcat, even though that cat could literally eat the dog alive in any showdown battle. In fact, in the unlikely event an unarmed human should come face to face with a bobcat in open country, the best thing for him to do is to start barking like a dog as loudly as he can and make a rush at the cat. The cat will invariably turn tail and run. You can bet your life on it. Which is exactly what you'll be doing.

Cornered or treed cats behave in quite a uniform manner. They will put their backs against some supporting protection and then can face their enemies head on. They will emit deep-throated growls and punctuate these growls with lusty spats. If the antagonist, be it man or dog, crowds them to the point of making them uneasy, they'll feint an attacking charge. This move generally covers no more than a couple of inches. But it is so convincing and so frightening that it invariably results in the antagonist backing off to a safer distance, giving the cat some breathing space.

If two opponents have a bobcat trapped between them and the cat can't get his back against some protective cover, his temper will quickly reach the explosive stage. With his head switching from side to side rapidly and his ears flicking like mad, he will try to keep track of both his tormentors. But his nerves will rapidly and suddenly become totally frazzled. Then he will do one of two things. If possible, he'll feint out both opponents and break into a run for escape. Or, he'll feint out one opponent, suddenly whirl and attack the other. More often than not, if he is crowded closely, he will choose the latter course of action. And the dogs stand no chance at all, unless they happen to be extremely huge dogs with tremendously powerful jaws.

Despite their sharp claws and blinding speed, bobcats are relatively fragile. Their bones are weak, their skulls are thin and, like most other members of the cat family, are more apt to avoid a showdown fight than seek one. Even the cat heavyweights, like the jaguars and the cougars, which can weigh upwards of 225 pounds, would rather "switch than fight." They much prefer game they can overwhelm by surprise attack; they avoid opponents that can supply them with a drag-out fight.

About the only time that untrapped bobcats may go on the offensive is when someone or something is trying to take fresh-killed game away from them. At those times, even a close approach may cause their tempers to flare up into raging fury. Humans finding themselves in such a situation should merely back off slowly, keeping the cat in front of them. To turn and run may more than likely encourage the cat to make a food-defending charge.

The bobcat hasn't overpopulated its hunting areas simply because of its low rate of reproduction. The usual litter is two, although young females may sometimes only deliver a single kitten. The female chooses dry surroundings, such as caves and nests under windfalls, for her nursery den. Since the new-born kittens are blind and helpless, they stay with their mother until they're yearlings. During this time they acquire self-protection and hunting knowledge.

As with many other species, the male has absolutely no paternal interest in his brood. In fact, if the female should leave the den to go hunting, he is just as apt to kill his young as not. That is one of the reasons why a female who has recently borne a litter is in such foul temper most of the time. Every intruder into the den is looked upon as a potential murderer of her kittens. She will rarely wander more than a half mile from the den and the slightest whimper from her kittens will get her racing back.

Along with tracking with hounds, the most successful way of getting a yellow-eyed bobcat mounted for your trophy room is to use a call. The most effective call is the cry of a cottontail in distress. It is totally incongruous, but this otherwise secretive, crafty and highly intelligent animal is an absolute sucker for the sound of a predator call. And it is positively ridiculous in its reactions to this trick. There is no need to stay upwind from the direction in which the cat is coming toward you. The man scent won't deter it from slowly but surely coming in to the sound of the call. There isn't any need to seek cover or even to wear camouflage clothing. There have been many instances where cats have

CLOSE-RANGE PREDATOR CALL

actually walked up to within ten strides of the calling hunter.

You can use some of the excellent electronic calls on the market today or the old-fashioned mouth-blown calls. If you're in range of a bobcat's hearing, either or both will be equally effective. And, as noted earlier, you don't need any sophisticated armament. A simple light woods rifle will do beautifully.

The Lynx

The lynx can be considered an overgrown cousin to the bobcat. They resemble each other very closely, both having short, stubby tails and long legs. The surest way of telling them apart is by the coloring of the tip of the tail. Whereas the bobcat's is black on the top and sides, with either white or tan on the underside, the lynx's tip is black all around.

The lynx inhabits the northern forests of the United States and Canada, most of them being found in Canada. He moves silently on big, furry feet, has tufted ears and yellow eyes which are exceedingly alert while seeking prey. He wears a coat of smoky gray fluff and has an enormous ruff of hair framing his head. Unbelievable as it may be, he's even more elusive than the bobcat and can weigh upwards of 30 pounds.

Like the wildcat, his favorite dish is of the rabbit family, particularly the snowshoe rabbit. However, when absolutely driven to it by the scarcity of rabbits due to their ten-year cyclic decline in population, the lynx will add grouse, rodents and foxes to its diet. It'll even attack young mountain sheep, caribou fawns and even full-grown injured deer when forced to by extreme hunger.

Also much like the bobcat, the lynx can be attracted by a predator call. For this critter, it is best to use a type of call that imitates the deeper call of the jackrabbit rather than the high-pitched scream of the cottontail in dire distress. This varmint is also heavily hunted with hounds, especially in winter when his tracks may be easily followed in the snow.

The Cougar

There is still no closed season on the cougar in many states and that's why we're including him here. In fact, they are an endangered species and even those who hunt them most are fighting to protect them as game animals. Several Western states have responded to this by putting the cougar on the protected list, with hunting allowed only during the open season. So check the game laws of the state in which you are hunting before going out after this critter.

This large cat goes by many names: puma, painter, catamount, mountain lion, and panther. The fact remains, however, that no matter what it is called, the cougar is larger by far than any other species of cat in the United States. The range of this animal covers a vast portion of the North American continent. This range includes the area from central Canada through the United States and on into Mexico. It is in Mexico that the cougar does not rate as the largest feline; here his supremacy is supplanted by that spotted beauty . . . the jaguar. Nevertheless, the cougar is a large cat. Many specimens attain a length of eight feet from nose to tail-tip and achieve a weight of 225 pounds. This is no house pet. Cougars have a tawny beauty, with coat colorations varying according to environment and including shades of brown-gray and running through to a vibrant rust. Their tails are dark-tipped and average about 30 inches in length.

These large cats are strictly carnivorous and will cover tremendous distances while seeking food. They prey in most instances upon deer, and in so doing, they serve to maintain a balance in nature by culling out the aged and infirm members of the antlered tribe. This leaves the superior animals to breed and continue the species. It is when the cougar begins to kill domestic livestock and poultry that he runs into trouble with ranchers and farmers. Such predations cause him to be designated as a varmint and he is thereby hunted down and slain for his misjudgment.

When it is necessary to go after a rogue cougar, most varminters use hounds that have been trained specifically as lion dogs to trail the big cats and bring him to bay. Cougars are ferocious, efficient killers. Though reluctant to fight, they are capable of inflicting terrible punishment and even death upon a careless dog.

Cougar hunting is generally done on horseback because of the great distances covered in the chase. Therefore, most varminters carry a saddlegun of .30-.30 caliber. Others prefer a handgun using magnum loads.

Chapter 10
The Power Mower

The woodchuck is such an industrious agricultural pest that he can be referred to as an animated power mower. He keeps his belly comfortably stuffed with the very juiciest greenery he can find. He is such an aggressive agricultural pest that farmers warmly welcome any responsible hunter who wishes to clear their pastures of these destructive varmints.

Rodents are the most widely hunted varmints in all of North America. The woodchuck, which is definitely a member of the rodent family, is far and away the most popular quarry. And no varmint has been so important in so many ways in developing the art of hunting the pest species as has this critter. As the crow has become the king of avian targets for shotguns, so the woodchuck has become the king of furry varmints for riflemen.

The American population of woodchucks, also known as groundhogs, whistlers, marmots and pasture-pigs,, is estimated to be in the hundreds of millions. Add to this the fact that they are not the easiest targets to hit and you realize that there is very little chance that they can ever be rendered extinct by varmint hunters.

The extent of the groundhog's habitat is vast, covering most of the contiguous United States and on into Canada; from Alaska in the west his range extends eastward to Labrador. As among most species of animals there seems to be an area more favored than others. And so it is with the woodchuck clan. This varmint is found in greatest profusion in the northeastern portion of the country. This territory encompasses the area from Virginia, West Virginia, and Maryland, northward to Maine.

In his feeding habits, the woodchuck somewhat parallels the prairie dog in that he doesn't pay too much attention to water. He satisfies his thirst by concentrating on succulent, juicy grub. He does quite a bit of travelling in his search for desirable food. He doesn't go any great distances, just far enough to give him a varied and well-balanced diet.

As he travels along finding his feed, the woodchuck keeps himself quite busy. Using well-developed front claws, he digs many burrows to keep himself safe from natural and human predation while he stays close to his pastural pantry.

Where he digs his burrows depends mostly on the type of territory he's in at the time. Where soft loam is most prevalent, he generally will dig among the entwining roots of fairly good-sized shrubs and trees. This makes it more difficult for digging enemies to find and invade his motel-type home. Where the soil is cluttered with rocks, he will usually dig under or between rock slabs or deeply bedded stones. In other words, he uses the terrain of the area in which he happens to be to his best advantage.

Chucks are most active during the balmy months of spring and early summer. During this time, they raise their young and extend their range of resting burrows as soon as the youngsters are about one-third grown. It is at this time of year that they offer the eager varmint hunters the greatest number of targets.

However, when the weather turns sizzling hot in late summer and early autumn, woodchucks become quite scarce. They've usually already put on all the body lard they need to serve them through their winter hibernation. Also these creatures have a very low tolerance of extremely hot, dry weather. Besides, their favorite sources of nourishment have grown dry and tasteless and are no longer the lure for gorgings.

It is also during this time of the year that chucks try out dens for the coming winter's hibernation. This is known as their siesta period. To be suitable, dens must remain cool and comfortable during the weeks-long siesta, and, of course, be below the frost line. If a particular den proves to be unsuitable for hibernation, the canny little rodent merely travels a bit to another one of the considerable number of hideouts that were fashioned during the earlier, more idyllic days and tries out another den.

Inexperienced, unknowledgeable hunters who don't know about the woodchuck's habit of taking long siestas during the dog-days of late summer are caught by surprise by the sudden absence of these varmint targets. Many a weekend hunter has been embarrassed by this woodchuck disappearing act. He goes out one weekend and sees loads of targets. So, he invites some of his friends out for a varminting fiesta the following week. But during the intervening week the weather has turned intolerably hot and dry for the little pests and they've gone underground to start their siesta. Comes Saturday and Sunday and our hunting neophyte can be made to feel awfully foolish trying to find some targets for himself and his friends. Actually, at this time the targets are so far underground that it would take artillery of considerable size to reach them.

The varmints wind up their siesta period in late autumn, just before the onset of honest-to-goodness winter. They emerge from their chosen dens for the last feeding orgy and also to carry in some sun-dried grasses with which to fashion crude nests to help warm them during the hibernation period. Except during a protracted Indian Summer, the fall feeding appearance lasts about two or three weeks and that's generally all you'll see of woodchucks until the following spring.

Of course, some chucks do emerge from hibernation during the bitter-cold weather of winter. But these are the woeful beasts that are doomed in any one of several ways. They may be so beset by parasites that they emerge in a vain attempt to escape extreme discomfort; they may have miscalculated and didn't lay on a sufficient layer of lard to keep them comfortably insulated during their long sleep; they may have chosen unwisely (not all chucks are brilliant) when picking out their hibernating quarters and are attempting to avoid freezing to death by looking for another den. No matter what the reason, the chuck who emerges from his den at this time of year usually dies from what has come to be known as "natural" causes.

Woodchucks are to be found in extremely varied locations, from the high grassy mountain basins down to hot and humid areas that are only about ten to twenty feet above sea level. The varieties of the marmot clan and the names by which they are known are as diverse as the places they range.

It is in the farming areas of the Northeast states that he wreaks the greatest havoc upon the agricultural community. Being an indiscriminate feeder, he nonetheless seems to choose his diet from among the choice, neatly planted rows of truck farms. However, this is not to say that berry bushes, fruit orchards and hay fields are overlooked. His appetite for vegetation is enormous and it is upon such a diet that he prospers.

Truck farmers, whose financial lives are dependent on the growing of vegetable produce, particularly look with great disfavor on the woodchuck. Chucks have a maniacal enthusiasm for mowing down juicy vegetables such as lettuce, cabbage and cauliflower. They also like to take healthy bites out of the top growth of many root vegetables. For dessert, these pests go for peas and beans, especially in the tender stages of growth. No, sir. Groundhog Day is not celebrated with any degree of gaiety in truck-farming communities.

Believe it or not, this voracious destroyer of pasture and farmlands does serve a useful purpose . . . but not for mankind. Cottontails are regularly benefitted by the talent of the chucks as housing engineers. Where cottontails make up a high proportion of huntable small game, the chucks' dens many times prove to be the salvation of the small, sweet-meated rabbits. They use the burrows dug by chucks to escape from human and animal predation. Especially in bitter cold weather, which cottontails cannot tolerate for any extensive periods, the chucks' dens offer a snug retreat.

At higher elevated timberlines, the woodchuck is known as the "whistler." When a woodchuck becomes aware of the presence of a hunter and feels endangered, he'll emit a loud, shrill whistle which alerts every other chuck in the area. These high-elevation woodchucks are also referred to as marmots. Some of them sport a shoulder cape of hair that is slightly longer than, and of a contrasting color to, the rest of their hairy pelt. These capes somewhat resemble mantles. But, whatever they are called and whether or not they wear mantles, they all have the same husky body, the same badgerlike digging habits and the same voracious appetites that distinguish the entire rodent clan.

The woodchuck is certainly not the handsomest of varmints but he does have a certain quizzical charm. A description of the animal would go something like this: It has a short, rounded head that is broad in structure and tufted with dark bristles of hair. The head is set firmly on a corpulent body that appears too wide for its height. The eyes are well set, relatively small but efficient. About one-fifth of the creature is taken up by a rather flat, densely-haired tail.

The front legs are a good deal longer and with sharper claws. These are intended for rapid and efficient digging of new burrows and for cleaning out the debris that has accumulated in old hideouts. As can be judged from his stocky body, the chuck is no great shakes as a speedster. A man running at the speed of a medium jog can easily keep up with a chuck running at full speed.

However, he is no slouch when it comes to rough-and-tumble fighting. Not that he goes out looking for trouble. On the contrary. He is most unlikely to attack man or dog even when cut off from his den.

But if a fight becomes unavoidable, as when he's crowded too closely, he won't back away. By using his bucky-beaverlike teeth and sharp front paws he can teach an inexperienced dog a trick or two about in-fighting. Of course, this relatively small rodent doesn't stand much of a chance against the much larger meat-eaters like the fox and coyote.

Young chucks are born when cold winter weather gives way to warm temperatures. Therefore, they are delivered at different times of the year, depending on where their mothers are living at the time. In the Mid-Atlantic and lower New England states, they generally come forth late in April or early in May. Down in the more southern states, they come earlier; in the northern states, where cold weather hangs around a bit longer, they may be born as late as the end of June. The litters vary in size depending on the species, but they average from four to six.

Woodchucks, being creatures of the open forest, fields and farmlands, have exceptionally keen eyesight. Also, the position of their eyes gives them a sort of periscopic view. This permits them to see what's going on while they hide just below the surface of their burrow entrance.

Their sense of hearing is so sharp the faintest sound will instantly put them on guard. Once a chuck sees you, you can't fool him by trying to hide. The moment you get out of sight, he will dive for his burrow. There he'll patiently wait until he feels certain you've gone away.

Don't be careless in your stalking of these critters just because their sense of scent isn't as highly developed as their other senses. They are very sensitive to the ground vibrations set off by any heavy-footed hunter.

When out looking for places to hunt for chucks, keep a sharp eye out for mounds of earth piled outside their dens. Close-cropped grass runways leading from one mound to another is a good clue that chucks are in the neighborhood. These dirt mounds can generally be seen from a considerable distance and usually mean you can do your hunting that same day. However, it's a good idea to play a waiting game and scout around the day before you get down to serious shooting.

A mature woodchuck offers quite a hunk of target. His hide is tough enough that muleskinners used to use a strip of it as the "popper" at the tip of their whips. His body is made up of solid, muscular flesh. Most important of all, the critter has a tremendous will to live. He must be solidly and powerfully hit to be dropped in his tracks.

The wariness of woodchucks varies in direct proportion to the amount of hunting done in any particular area. Where they are seldom hunted, it's not at all unusual to see chucks posing at the entrances of their dens, at ranges as close as 20 yards. But they smarten up rapidly in areas where they are heavily hunted and shot at often. There they will rarely offer themselves as targets at much under 150 yards. Where hunter visibility is high, like in wide open areas, shots have to be taken at much longer ranges.

More than any other pest species, the woodchuck has been responsible for the development of varied varmint cartridges. The first of these was the tiny .22 Hornet which was originated, tested, and refined to its present stage during the early 1930's. There were two primary reasons why this cartridge was developed. First, there was a need for a small cartridge that was better in its stopping power than the .22 rimfire then in popular use for varmint hunting; secondly, it had to be cheap and easily reloaded so that quantity shooting could be done at minimum expense.

In addition to meeting these two requirements, the .22 Hornet has a sound level low enough that it is seldom objected to by landowners on whose property woodchucks are shot. Also, it reduced the hazard of free-flying bullets in the densely populated areas of eastern and New England states. Misses result in disintegration of the tiny 45-grain bullets on the ground, against rocks and even against shrubbery backstops.

The term "varmint rifle" can be most misleading. Unfortunately, many woodchuck hunters learn this the hard, expensive way. We'll try to teach you how to properly choose armament easily and cheaply.

The first thing you have to learn and fully realize is that there is no one gun which is perfect for all species of pests and at every range. Choosing the wrong weapon for the kind of shooting you will be doing in your part of the country may simply mean the waste of the purchase price.

In order to get the right caliber for most of your chuck hunting, varmint rifles must be broken down into three classifications: for close-range, or intermediate-range, or long-range hunting. Distances of up to 250 yards would be classed as close-range; intermediate-range would be from 250 to about 300 yards; over 300 yards to the maximum of about 450 yards would fall into the long-range category. In the selection of a chuck caliber, consideration must be given not only to the distance at which most of your shooting will be done, but also that the gun is properly chambered for the particular cartridge you will be using.

One important point to bear in mind is that the little pesty woodchuck is deceptively tough to kill. Better to misjudge a bit on the too much power side than on the too little. If you're going to be shooting your chucks within 150 yards, the .22 Hornet should be used. Effective calibers for ranges from 150 to 250 yards include the .222, .222 magnum and the .223. Like the .22 Hornet, these loads have a relatively low noise level and at these distances are extremely accurate and powerful enough to get the job done.

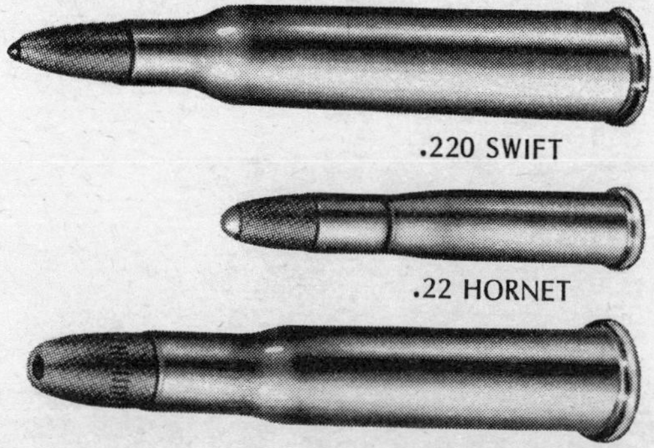

.220 SWIFT

.22 HORNET

30-30 WINCHESTER

Once you get into the intermediate range, you're pretty well limited to the .224 Weatherby magnum, the .225 Winchester and the .22/250 Remington. Of course, these cartridges perform extremely well at close range. But you don't need their power at short distances and they make far more noise than the previously mentioned loads. Especially if the hunting area in your community is divided into small lots by dwellings, roads, fences, woods, etc., don't pick one of these calibers. You'll simply be making a host of enemies for yourself unnecessarily because of the excessive noise. These three cartridges really come into their own out past 250 yards and which one you choose depends on what make of gun you want. Incidentally, for precision shooting at small targets, bolt-actions are the preferred type of rifle.

For the really avid sportsman who likes to do his shooting at long range, the .243 or .244 is preferred over anything else. These two cartridges are truly superb for their killing power at great distances, their wind-bucking ability, and their inherent accuracy. They are both effective up to about 450 yards and there aren't many varminters who can hit critters at this distance with any degree of consistency.

BUSHNELL 1.5X-4X SCOPECHIEF V RIFLESCOPE

BUSHNELL 3X-9X SCOPECHIEF V RIFLESCOPE

BUSHNELL 4X SCOPECHIEF V RIFLESCOPE

If most of your shooting is done at less than 250 yards, you can get by with a 4X scope, although a 6X or 8X is better. The fact is, the lower the power, the easier it is to keep the cross hairs steady. And for varminting, nothing but a cross hair scope should be used. The other reticle styles are suitable for big-game hunting but they just aren't fine enough for the precision work called for in varminting. Beyond 250 yards, a 4X or 6X scope becomes a handicap because the cross hairs will cover too much of the target. An ideal scope for close-range and intermediate-range shooting is a 3X-9X or 2X-10X variable.

Of course, if you're one of those fellows who thinks he would like to shoot at varmints running around in the next county, be prepared to part with a good deal of money for a target scope and adjustable mounts . . . and get ready to conquer an extremely powerful instrument, with cross hairs that will leap off the target every time your heart beats. Controlling a 14X or stronger scope takes a heck of a lot of practice plus a rifle that has a trigger pull of no more than about 2½ pounds.

One of the most outstanding characteristics of the woodchuck is

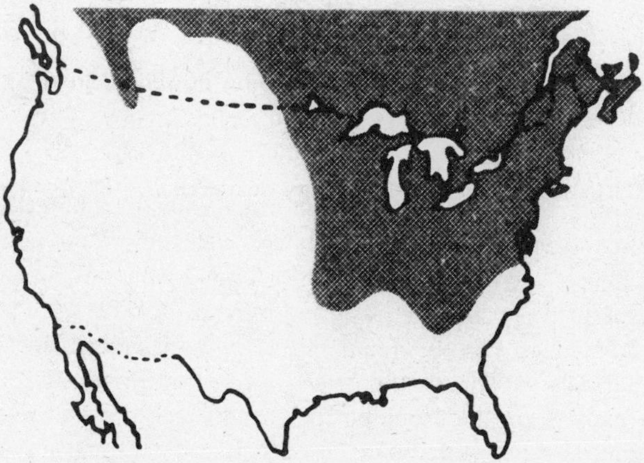

WOODCHUCK RANGE

its ability to withstand shock. These varmints, with their muscular bodies, just don't seem to know when they've been killed. Therefore, it is smart to place your shots very carefully and get the most out of your expenditure on ammo by shooting at ranges that are proper for the caliber you're using.

If you are hunting on foot, pick out a likely looking field and examine it thoroughly through binoculars. Walk slowly and do a lot of looking. If you're cruising along roads in a car, keep a watchful eye out for fields that are pocked by holes and mounds of dirt. Also, look for chucks themselves. If you should spot a potential target, pick out a good shooting site. This should offer a clear shot, preferably one that you can make from the prone position, and check the area where the bullet could carry if you should miss. You don't want to risk hitting any livestock.

Without unduly hurrying and drawing attention to yourself, get into the steadiest shooting position you can and take careful aim. Hold for the neck, head or upper body, deliberately squeeze off the shot . . . and immediately get another cartridge into the chamber. If you've hit the chuck and he moves, shoot again before he has a chance to get down into his burrow.

Strangely enough, should you miss him entirely, it's likely that he'll give you another crack at him. These varmints are not always greatly disturbed by shots fired from 200 or more yards away, even if the bullet should strike quite close. Somehow, they don't seem to relate the sound of the shot to the landing of the slug. If the target does jump into his hole, hold steady for a few minutes. These are generally very curious beasties and they'll often come up again to see what all the noise is about.

Woodchucks should be treated as superb sport. They are far too important to the economy of American varmint hunters to be treated otherwise. True, they must be hunted down when they become too numerous and interfere with man's use of the land he lives on. But they deserve to be killed cleanly in the most humanitarian manner that accurate rifles, powerful-enough cartridges and the best possible marksmanship can provide.

Chapter 11
Starlings and Sparrows

Various small birds have multiplied to such great populations that they are giving fits to farmers, urban dwellers and suburban residents all over the country. One of the most disliked of this category is the starling, which is strongly cussed wherever there are people to do the cussing.

These winged pests are relatively quite small and, individually, make somewhat difficult targets. However, they usually fly in huge flocks so that when you do get to hit one, you'll probably hit one or two others along with it.

This bird has absolutely nothing desirable about him. Yet, some unknown European introduced him to this country, probably with the laudable intention of sharing some birds he had known in the old country with his new American friends. He would have done us all a much greater favor if he had left the starling in its native habitat.

Starlings must rank high on the list of the filthiest, most useless and most troublesome of nature's creatures. They eat tremendous amounts of grain and as if that weren't enough, they also damage great numbers of growing grain crops, fruits and berries. They don't even bother to keep their quarters clean. On the contrary, their nests generally reek of putrefaction, not only from dropped bits of food left to rot but from the stinking, irremovable droppings of the young birds.

Busy, heavily-populated midtown areas don't easily escape the scourge of starlings, either. When winter comes, these nuisances find

that their summer roosts become quite uncomfortable. So they seek the warmer comforts of the inner city. During the relatively balmy though cool days of autumn, they take up residence in the many-branched trees of residential communities. Since starlings are a very close-knit breed and like each other's company to the point of grouping together by the hundreds and sometimes thousands, their chattering can be quite a source of irritation to suburban dwellers, especially during the night. And it doesn't soothe that irritation much when you get up in the morning to find you have to hose down your walk to free it of starling droppings. And worse than that inconvenience is the damage these birds do to automobiles. Their droppings are slimy and acidic and do fearful things to car finishes. They eat into the finish with such speed that, if not removed within an hour or two, these droppings can cut through the finish down to the metal itself. It doesn't take much more than an overnight bombing to make a brand-new car look as though it had been hit by a load of buckshot.

As the winter goes into its colder portion, these pests find that office buildings offer better windbreaks. And perching on ledges and windowsills while enjoying the heat given off by these buildings sure beats sitting out on bare tree branches, buffeted by icy blasts of winter wind. Neither the hustle and bustle of downtown traffic nor the glow of street lights below them deter them from invading these business districts in droves. And here their drop bombings can reach massive proportions. The honk of a car's horn, a screech of brakes, or the opening of several office windows could startle these birds and set off a shower onto the passersby below. And the starling dropping is a messy bit of elimination. It doesn't simply hit and bounce away . . . it splatters. Wherever the birds' population grows to large numbers and they can find enough food to support them within easy reach, this inundation occurs. Especially in Midwestern cities, which are on the edges of farm and tree country, it is not unusual to see diners, theatergoers, and others walking downtown streets wearing rubbers and carrying umbrellas . . . on clear, moonlit winter nights.

There is, however, one characteristic about this pest that is truly beautiful. Except during the nesting season, they always fly in huge flocks. While they look extremely clumsy and awkward when on the ground, they are something else again in the air. It is really marvelous to watch them flush, wheel, and glide in massed precision flight. It is almost as though all the birds were controlled by one master flight instrument, all activated at the same instant.

Starlings are small, chunky, square-tailed birds. At a distance, they appear to be jet-black in color but they actually have an iridescent plumage spotted with grayish dots. Fledglings are somewhat iron-gray in color. During the spring, which is their mating and nesting season, their pointed bills are yellow.

In addition to their ceaseless noise and the filth of their droppings and their destruction of so much of farmers' crops, these birds have proven to be a downright menace to modern-day America. The most dramatic illustration of this occurred in October 1960.

One day, a four-engine prop-jet Electra roared down Runway 9 of Logan Airport outside of Boston, Massachusetts. There were 67 passengers and 5 crew members aboard as the plane took off, bound for Atlanta, Georgia. Just seconds later, the plane faltered, turned its nose down, and splashed into a channel of Boston harbor. The final count was 62 dead of the 72 who had taken off just seconds before.

The official cause of this fatal disaster was a small flock of starlings. FAA investigators, called to the scene almost immediately, found a number of dead birds on the runway; rescue workers found bits of birds and feathers stuck to parts of the ill-fated plane. After intensive investigation of all the facts, the FAA reported that the immediate reason for the crash was loss of flying power as the plane took off. This was caused, not by true mechanical failure, but by a flock of starlings that had been sucked into the plane's turbine engines as the plane roared down the runway for its takeoff.

This is but one example of but one problem caused by today's tremendous starling population. There are cases on record where the droppings of these birds, in certain areas, have provided perfect incubating places for disease spores. This has led to serious illness and even death in a great many young children.

These birds have become so abundant that they are ruinous to crops and hazardous to humans. And so, despite the feeling of fanatic bird lovers that everything wearing feathers is sacred, we don't consider starlings among our fine-feathered friends. They are nobody's friend.

Another bird which has become a pest is the sparrow, but not as seriously as the starling because the all-too-familiar sparrow is not truly hazardous to humans. The sparrows have become pests only because there are so very many of them. They have simply become nuisances.

These birds are distributed so widely and are so well known that there is no need to describe them here. Like the starling, they were originally imported to North America. Sometime around 1800, an Englishwoman sent two pairs to her son who had emigrated to America. She wanted him to have some of the bird sounds of his homeland about him so he wouldn't be too homesick. Unfortunately, the young man had an ear for music and the shrill, noisy chirps of the sparrows proved to be anything but soothing. He didn't have the heart to destroy them so he simply turned them loose.

These previously caged birds proved to be quite hardy and perfectly capable of existing and, indeed, thriving as free-wheeling members of the avian clan. In the century or so since they were first intro-

duced into this country, they have come to cover this land like a blanket.

They are highly gregarious, congregating in huge, noisy flocks. That is, except when nesting. At that time, they have many squabbles while competing for nesting sites and building materials and food. Frequently, these robber-birds will brazenly move in and take over birdhouses that have been put up for better-mannered and sweeter-voiced members of the bird species. These strong-beaked nuisances have so saturated available habitat that they have, in many areas, driven off more desirable birds.

Like the starling, they are just as much at home in urban centers as they are in agricultural surroundings. Thanks to that doting Englishwoman and her tender-eared son, there is no building, tree, fence, or any other likely perch anywhere in the United States free of their communal roosts. Vine- and flower-covered walls are special favorites of theirs.

These English sparrows are so prevalent that they are almost ignored as a pest species. But they constantly feed on grain seeds, grass seeds, fruits, and seed-vegetables throughout the year. Out in rural areas, poultry and other livestock many times find it difficult to get enough to eat because of flocks of sparrows swarming in at feeding time. While each individual bird eats very little at each meal, there are so many birds and so many meals that the annual feed bill for them is truly tremendous.

Other birds that fall into the pest category because of their ruinous effect on the economic health of farmers across the country are blackbirds, grackles and cowbirds. Their populations have grown to such proportions that, regardless of what fanatic bird lovers may say to the contrary, these birds should be destroyed whenever and wherever possible.

Of course, it is impossible to go gunning for them in well-populated urban and suburban areas. However, out in the rural countryside, go get them. Any shotgun will do. If you have a 12-gauge, use a standard field load and go out and get yourself some practice. For a little more difficult shooting, test your skill with a .22-caliber shotgun. A 20-gauge with a modified choke, loaded with express shells carrying one ounce of No. 9 shot, will do very nicely for the average shotgunner.

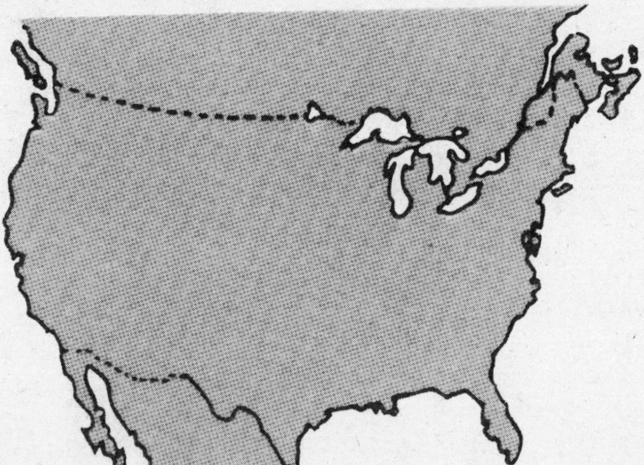

SPARROW RANGE

Chapter 12
Other Furred Pests

Although they are not considered too high on the list of varmints, gophers and jackrabbits are among the most popular attractions for varmint hunters. These members of the rodent species are so widely and generously distributed that they have come to be known as the child's and poor man's varmints. No fancy gear or extraordinary skill is required to hunt them effectively. You can have just as much sport with them, armed with nothing more than a .22 rifle and hunting eagerness as the sophisticated hunter with his superaccurate, highiy expensive equipment who scorns anything less than long-range shots. These rodents provide most satisfactory targets to all, especially the young boy just starting to hunt.

Technically speaking, gophers are really ground squirrels. But the terms are so interchangeable, depending on what part of the country you're in, that for the purpose of this discussion we'll call them gophers.

North American gophers are to be found chiefly in the prairies and on open mountain slopes, covering an area that ranges from the Arctic coast of Alaska and Canada as far south as the deep valleys of Mexico. They are also found in relatively large numbers in heavily farmed regions. However, they leave the heavily forested areas of the continent fairly well barren of their presence.

They are found in great numbers most frequently in pastures, fields of hay, and along the edges of croplands. In the spring, before grasses and crops have grown to any appreciable height, they are wide open to observation. Later on, grazing, haying and harvesting also leave them very much exposed to the hunter's eyes. In this way nature has enabled us to efficiently hunt these rodents during most of the spring, summer, and early fall.

Although determined by a not-too-scientifically-approved formula, gophers, or ground squirrels,can be split into four major categories. The divisions are here set up by the comparative lengths of their tails and the differences in their living habits.

The first of these divisions is the 13-striped spermophile. These are truly tiny gophers who get their name from the stripes running the length of them. They are found in greatest numbers in relatively dry, grassy prairie regions on both sides of the Missouri River. Very rarely are they seen east of the Mississippi.

As with all the other members of the ground squirrel family, the best time of year to hunt these little stripers is during the early spring. Just as the grass starts to turn green, they can be seen at quite some distance. The next best time is right after hayfields are mowed. Then the gophers are highly visible on the clipped grass. Of course, there's also fine hunting in pastures which livestock keep flattened throughout the summer.

When summer is gone and all seed-bearing plants are ripened, these little pests are busy as can be storing up all the seed they can find.

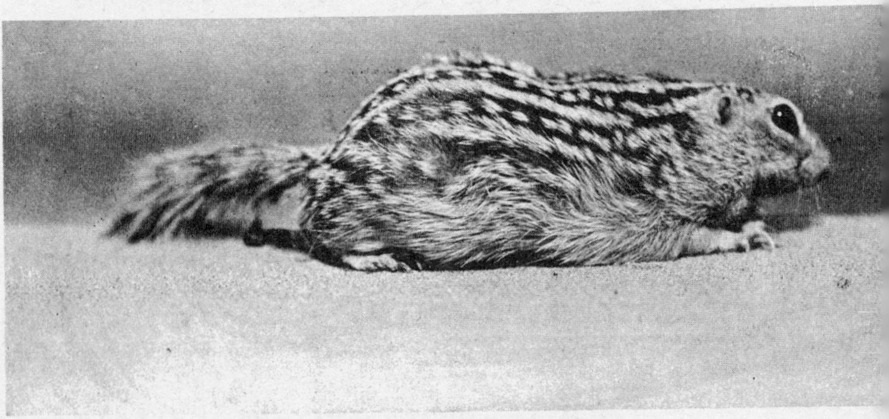

THIRTEEN-STRIPED SPERMOPHILE

This is the start of the lean part of the year as far as hunting these animals is concerned.

These 13-striped spermophiles are different from their related species in more than just coloring and size. They are the best camouflaged and the smallest. They are also far less gregarious than all the other divisions of the gopher clan. That is, they don't live in close harmony with their own kind and form community villages. Their burrows are widely separated from each other, even where there are loads of them in any given area. And their burrows don't have any mounds of dirt around the entrances to indicate their existence. It's not at all unusual to see one running across a blank piece of land, stop still for an instant, and suddenly disappear, as if into thin air.

A striper who has been frightened into diving down its tube into the underground will often give off an unusually high-pitched, trembling, long-drawn-out whistle-like sound. They'll never do this above ground, as though unwilling to call attention to themselves while still in a vulnerable position. In many ways, the striper is in a class all its own.

FLICKERTAIL

The second division of gophers is made up of the Richardson or flickertail. These gophers, beside being somewhat longer, are about four times larger in girth than the little stripers. They are also far more community-minded and are, therefore, easier to find. However, they are far more wary as rifle targets.

Their popular name of "flickertail" derives from their habit of posing in an upright position at the entrance of their den, emitting short, shrill whistles. And each time they whistle, they jerk, or flicker, their tails. Much like the prairie dog, these gophers like roomy dens built in close commune with others of their own kind. Some communities of these gophers have been spotted on plateaus as high as 10,000 feet above sea level in the Rocky Mountain ranges. At lower elevations, where the once-arid land has been irrigated into good, producing cropland, these pests oftentimes become quite numerous and very destructive to a wide range of crops.

The third division, which includes the ring-tailed and the Goldman's forms, are all marked by tails that are thick-haired and range from six to about ten inches in length.

The fourth and, for our purposes, the last division of the gopher clan have a hair coloring that is far more appealing than that of the others. These gophers very much resemble chipmunks in that they are very nervous little rodents. They tend to carry their tail high in the air when in full flight, and are extremely adept tree climbers. They eat their meals in the trees and shrubs that manage to grow in their dry habitat. However, like all the others of their species, they live in holes in the ground, preferably where there is some rock protection at the entrances of their dens.

One natural trait is common with all gophers. They are highly efficient and industrious savers. While the weather is fine and crops are plentiful, they harvest seeds and berries and nuts of many varieties. These they store in underground dens so they won't go hungry during inclement weather or, in northerly climates, during the winter months.

Naturally, gophers that congregate in communities provide far more excellent quantity hunting than do the forms that are less gregarious. However, villagers are far more wary and most often have to be shot at ranges of 75 yards or more. At that range, the .22 rimfire cartridges are somewhat less than ideal, especially on such small targets.

The most popular among gopher hunters are the .222 and its magnum big brother, with the highly accurate 6 mm twins, the .243 and .244, not far behind in popularity.

The jackrabbit is probably the most popular target of all in the western plains states. Biologically speaking, the jackrabbit is not a rodent but a lagamorph. But don't try to convince a hunter of this scientific fact. To him, the jackrabbit has always been, is, and always will be a rodent. And since most states don't have any closed season on these critters, they are always available.

The North American jackrabbit is subdivided into two separate species. These branches of the clan are classified as the whitetail and the blacktail. Whitetails inhabit the more northern sectors of the United States and on into Canada. The blacktails are the southern cousins and they inhabit a range which encompasses the American Southwest and extends into Mexico. There is an overlap of the two species along an approximately 60 mile-wide strip of the area which borders South Dakota and Nebraska.

While each of the rabbits has several subspecies, it takes a scientifically trained zoologist's eye to tell the difference. For all intents and purposes, all the whitetails are pretty much alike. At maturity, their

JACKRABBIT

weight averages between six and eight pounds and they are about 22 inches long. One of their distinguishing characteristics is, as their name implies, a white tail; another hallmark is their black ear tips. During the winter, when snow carpets much of their range, nature endows them with a completely white coat, but strangely, their ears remain tipped in black.

Blacktails remain a uniform, smoky-gray color throughout the entire year. They average from four to six pounds in weight, although their body length is approximately the same as that of the whitetail. These physical characteristics give them a somewhat slim and leaner look than their whitetail counterparts.

Not only are these two different in coloring, they are also quite different in their running habits. During warm-weather months, when heavy cover conceals them extremely well, whitetails will most often hold in place until a hunter is within just a few feet of them. Then they'll get up and run at an almost leisurely and bouncy gait for 50 to 100 yards, as though they were challenging the hunter to a chase. At that point, they'll suddenly settle down to a flatter, speedier pace and try to put considerable distance between themselves and whatever it was that disturbed them before seeking covering shelter in which to rest.

This habit of waiting for the last moment before leaving cover changes in the winter months, especially when snow is late in arriving. Then the pure-white covering of their fur leaves them embarrassingly well-exposed to the hunter's eye. They seem to know that they are now more readily seen, and they become increasingly wary and usually take off out of their thin cover while a hunter may still be as much as 50 yards away. This increased wariness remains with them throughout the winter. When the snow is crusted and quite hard, it will have a tendency to crunch under the feet of an approaching hunter. This sound is easily picked up by the jackrabbit's sensitive ears and he may jump into headlong flight at ranges of 100 yards or more.

Blacktails, on the other hand, maintain the same habit all year long. They'll usually hold cover until the hunter is within 20 to 30 yards before breaking. But when they do break, it's not in any leisurely, bouncy manner. They sail out in a headlong, racy sprint and keep it up until they have found some type of bulge in the earth's surface behind which to hide. This makes them highly prized as running rifle targets. Anyone who practices shooting at running blacktails long enough to become skillful at it usually becomes fairly expert shooting at foxes and coyotes as well as at big game like deer and antelope.

Whitetails generally bear one litter a year. In the southernmost regions of their range they may sometimes bear two. Blacktails, however, always bear two and quite frequently may bring forth three. The litters of both average four, though six is not unusual. The young are born fully furred and well-developed and are able to run and take fairly good care of themselves within just a few days after birth.

Blacktails' meat and fur have no commercial value at all. They are sometimes trapped to be used to train greyhounds and whippets for chasing coyotes. Other than that, their only value lies in the fact that they offer some fantastic sport and they are great for hunters practicing on running game.

The whitetails of the northern ranges, however, do have commercial value. Their pelts are used for making an inexpensive grade of felt; their meat is ground up and is either fed to penned fur-bearing animals or is sold as food for dogs and cats.

The blacktail jackrabbit is one of the most prolific animals on the North American continent. They rank as one of the two speediest animals on the great prairie lands. They are possibly exceeded only by the pronghorn antelope.

These jacks do not burrow for safety nor do they seek covering shelter once they have begun to run from danger. They rely solely on speed to put distance between them and their enemies. Their fur coloration allows them to blend so well into their surrounding cover that they will often sit so tight that a hunter walks right by them. But when they become frightened, they pop up literally at a hunter's feet and take off in a headlong run. And when they run, they run like the wind. With his tail down and his ears laid back flat against his head, a jackrabbit can accelerate to a speed of 40 miles an hour or better.

BOBCAT

WOODCHUCK

SNOWSHOE RABBIT

BLACK-TAILED JACKRABBIT

Bird shooters have, in their clay-pigeon games, such as trapshooting, a reasonable approximation of what they'll come up against in field shotgunning. Of course, there are no overhanging tree branches, shrubs, etc. but most of the variations in angle, speed, range and elevation can be duplicated with man-made targets. But nothing has ever been invented which does the same for the rifle hunter.

Nothing inanimate can ever duplicate the unpredictability of live game in the field. How can you manufacture the problems of an animal partially concealed in cover, camouflaged by nature's distinctive coloration, and taking advantage of contrasts in light and shadow? There just aren't any clay-pigeon games for riflemen that can duplicate the pressure of time, the excitement and the unpredictability of a wild animal, especially one on the run. No kind of artificial target can prepare a hunter for that crucial moment when a deer or other big-game breaks cover in a headlong dash for safety. Paper targets are better than nothing, but for real live-action practice, plus first-class sport, nothing beats the long-eared jackrabbits of the western prairies.

These critters are easily found in every state west of the Mississippi River, in five provinces of Canada and throughout Mexico and are the answer to a practice-hungry rifleman's prayers. Farmers have been carrying on a relentless battle with jackrabbits since the prairie states were settled. In addition to what they eat, these speedy devils also destroy and waste still more. There is absolutely no reason for not classifying them as varmints. And that's why landowners will more often than not welcome responsible riflemen with open arms when these hunters ask permission to shoot up the rabbit population.

These critters are such big eaters and such destroyers of rangeland grass that they present real competition to farm and range livestock for available feed. There should be no hesitancy or compunction on the part of varmint hunters about shooting them for sport. Since they are nocturnal feeders, the best time of day to hunt them is during the late afternoon and in the early morning. Then you can get them either coming from or going to their feeding grounds.

The jacks have an extremely well-developed sense of smell; also, the slightest overt move will spook them. However, if you remain in one position, it's quite possible that they may not spot you when they attempt to check you out. They are readily flushed from hiding, but be prepared for action. Be reminded that these long-eared speedsters move like lightning and your shot had better be fast and "on-the-money."

Jacks are most prolific breeders and there is just no danger of ever wiping them out. Besides getting in some of the best available practice, you're serving a very useful purpose when you hunt them.

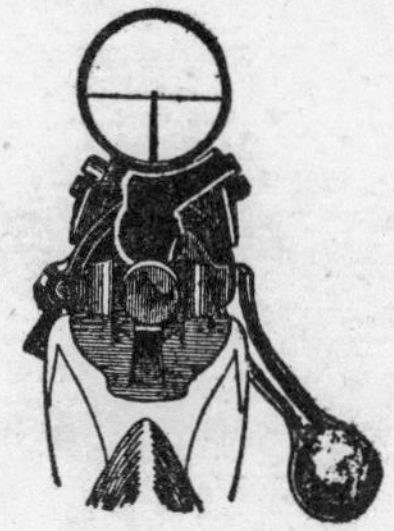

Chapter 13
Sighting-in Your Rifle

Sighting-in a rifle is nothing more than making sure your bullet goes where you aim it. Strange as it may seem, no one can properly sight a rifle for you . . . except you. Even without a shift in targets or an ammunition change, a rifle will rarely shoot to the same point of impact with different shooters. That is because no two shooters ever see the target the same way in the sights nor do any two people hold a rifle in exactly the same manner.

When should you sight-in your rifle? The first time will be as soon as possible after you get it. And it should be done with the ammunition you intend to use most often. With the passage of time, you may notice that your gun changes its point of impact somewhat. This means you will have to sight-in again if you want to maintain pin-point accuracy of your shots. Of course, re-sighting is necessary each time you change ammunition, even if the change is nothing more than just the brand. Most important of all, the wise hunter checks his rifle *before* a hunting trip.

When sighting-in your rifle, you should be either in the prone position or sitting at a sturdy bench or table. But don't ever use inflexible, sturdy objects such as posts, fence rails, logs, rocks, etc. for a forearm rest without laying some sort of soft padding under your forearm. Solid rests cause a rifle to shoot high. Then, when you hold the rifle without a rest, it probably will shoot too low.

The best place for sighting-in your rifle is a target range because

there the targets are set at measured distances.

Once you have sighted-in your rifle at a specific range, you should shoot at targets at other distances. This will help you to determine whether the bullet rises or falls. In sighting-in, think in terms of "groups" rather than bull's eyes. The latter are nothing more than a point of reference.

Ammunition can be saved by boresighting your rifle. There are mirror devices made for this purpose when firing lever, automatic or pump models. You can also use an optical boresighter. This method of sighting-in is particularly important when using a scope, which you will probably be doing most often when using a varmint rifle. If boresighting by eye, set your rifle on a support that is really steady, look through the bore and move the rifle until you see the target at dead center. The scope should then be adjusted by getting the cross hairs and the bore right on target.

To help you properly sight your rifle, scopes are fitted with windage and elevation adjustment knobs. These knobs are marked with arrows which indicate graduations and the direction in which you should move them so the bullet gets on target. Directions come packed with your scope which explain how much each graduation affects your shot.

A good binocular or spotting scope is helpful in spotting your shots on the target during sighting-in chores. Use great care in sighting your scope or iron sights during the process of sighting-in your rifle. Shoot as if each shot meant life or death. Sloppy shooting makes proper sighting-in impossible and is quite expensive in terms of ammunition used.

Chapter 14
Shotgun Hints

A shotgun is a weapon that discharges a relatively large number of pellets per load, covering a wide area of its target. Therefore, it would be reasonable to assume that even a shooter of only poor-to-fair skill should be able to master its use quite easily. Reasonable? Yes. Accurate? No. In actual practice, the acquirement of shotgun efficiency is one of the most difficult and mysterious problems in the entire field of firearms.

Most often, shotguns are used against moving targets. This type of shooting calls for the coordination of many factors: the ability to judge the initial speed of the load and its rate of speed reduction; the angle at which you're shooting and the speed of the target; the distance between the target and the shooter. These, and other variables such as wind drift, have to be carefully considered and computed in order to achieve the desired result—hitting the target.

As you squeeze the trigger, the load bursts from the end of your weapon at a high rate of speed. But once the load leaves the muzzle and is in free flight, its velocity is reduced by air friction. At really long range, this loss of velocity reaches such a degree that shooting at long range with a shotgun is a far more difficult skill to acquire than shooting within the more common range of approximately 40 yards.

Another variable factor to consider is the individual shooter's own reflexes. A gunner with lightning-fast reflexes can sometimes have his shot pattern hitting his target while his slower-shooting buddy is still squeezing the trigger of his weapon.

Also, the effects of wind and gravity on the spray patterns delivered by a shotgun have to be considered. Wind will deflect the pellets horizontally while gravity will pull them downward. So you can readily see that the load from a shotshell is subject, within its short range, to the same variable deflections that alter the course of rifle bullets which can reach much greater distances.

Strange as it may seem, shotguns, much like rifles, have a definite preference for some ammunition over other ammo. Two shotguns, built to the same specifications by the same manufacturer, much like twins, will rarely, if ever, perform identically. Under identical testing conditions, one is likely to deliver a much denser pattern than the other.

One of the commonest mistakes made by newcomers to the sport of shotgunning is that of using a size of shot too coarse for the game at which they're shooting. Commercially manufactured shotshells have standard weights of shot loaded into them. Therefore, there will be fewer pellets in a one-ounce load of coarse shot than in a similar load of finer shot. Naturally, the finer shot will give a denser pattern with its greater number of pellets. This automatically closes some of the "holes" which normally appear in the more open coverage of coarse shot. This, in turn, reduces the chances of game slipping through unhit. Beginning shotgunners sometimes make coarse-shot loads their choice in the mistaken belief that the best way to make clean kills is to hit their game with large-sized shot. They reason that larger shot sizes can drive more deeply into game and thus reach the vital area. In this reasoning they are manifestly correct, providing the game is hit with enough of these pellets.

However, there just aren't enough pellets in the coarse loads to plug "holes" in the pattern with any degree of uniformity. Under these circumstances, game is generally hit with less than killing density. Feathers may fly but the target goes on its way. When this happens, the result is often called a miss. Actually, it may just as easily be a crippling shot. If the wounds are truly minor, the game target will recover, although carrying those imbedded pellets for the rest of its life. However, if such wounds merely reach the vital areas without penetrating

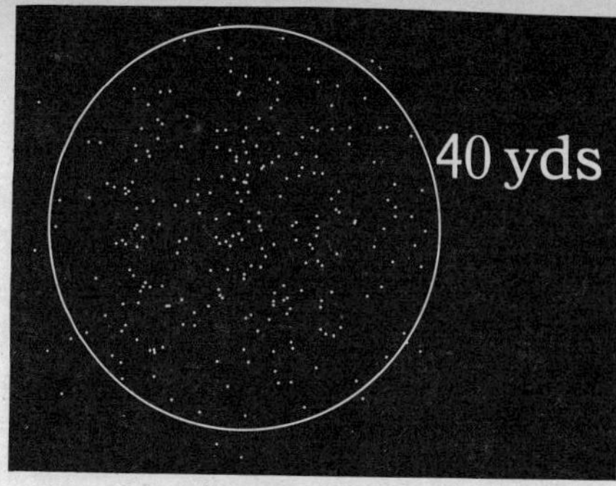

Pellet Size

No. Ounces	9	8	7½	6	5	4	2	BB
1⅞					318	252	168	93
1⅝				366	276	219	146	81
1½				337	256	203	135	
1⅜				309		186	124	69
1¼	731	513	438	281	213	169	113	63
1⅛	658	461	394	253	191	152	101	
1	585	410	350	225	170	135	90	
⅞	512	359		197	149	118		
¾	439		263	169	128	101		
½	293		175	113	85	68		

Choke	*Percentage of shot Within 30-Inch Circle at 40 Yards*
Full	65 to 75 per cent
Improved Modified	55 to 65
Modified	45 to 55
Improved Cylinder	35 to 45
Cylinder	25 to 35
Skeet	30 to 35

them deeply, the target may survive long enough to escape the hunter but soon after dies of its wounds.

In either event, the result is bad on two counts: the hunter doesn't collect his game and if the game should be classed as edible, such cripples reduce the supply of such game. In addition, such misuse of the shotgun results in needless, wasteful suffering by the game.

The experienced hunter frequently uses shot sizes smaller than those recommended by ammunition manufacturers for specific game because he finds the denser shot patterns more efficient. When using open-choked barrels, using fine-shot loads give an automatically denser pattern. In barrels with a tighter choke boring, this density of pellets often increases tremendously. And the denser the pattern, the greater the killing range.

The "choke" refers to the size of the opening at the muzzle which determines the distribution of shot or its spread. This is known as the gun's pattern. Chokes for shotguns come in five degrees. The cylinder bore is the most open of these. This choke is generally used on close-flushing game or on game taken at short range.

The improved cylinder boring is the next tighter degree of choke, followed by the modified, the improved-modified, and the full chokes. In addition to these, shotgun manufacturers also bore skeet chokes, which are special borings for skeet or clay-pigeon shooters.

When it comes to delivering tight and deadly patterns, most shotgunners aren't good enough marksmen to have this efficiency. Only the hunter who has the ability to coolly wait out targets that flush at short range until they are far enough away from his muzzle can use a full-choke shotgun efficiently. Otherwise, the game is mangled into a bloody mess by the dense shot load. But such patience is hard to find when the thrill of actual hunting has such a strong tendency to override the calm that is needed for functional field performance.

While sad, it is true that a great percentage of shotgunners don't use the right weapon to achieve good field performance. Most of those using full-choke shotguns haven't the ability to employ the fine efficiency of such borings; most of those using open-choke shotguns use them at distances beyond the efficient killing range of their wide-open patterns. Most of those in both groups would probably be much happier with themselves and their hunting by using shotguns bored with modified choke. Except for the most experienced and skillful, this is a good compromise.

The degree of choke is measured by the percentage of pellets which are shot into a 30-inch circle at 40 yards. However, choke dimensions are not really standard among the different manufacturers of guns. When you also consider the great differences in loads commonly used, you can more readily understand why guns seldom pattern according to choke charts. The only sure way to determine the constriction at the muzzle end of your gun is to pattern it.

Pin a large sheet of paper to some solid background support. Fire a round at the paper from a marked-off distance of exactly 40 yards. Then draw a circle 30 inches in diameter enclosing the greatest number of pellet holes. The next part is the hardest because it's the most tedious, but it must be done. Count the number of holes within the circle. Dividing the pellet table figure (see chart on p. 159) into the number of holes in the circle will give you the percentage that determines the degree of choke of your gun.

Let's illustrate this a bit further. Let us assume that a 12-gauge shell loaded with 1-1/8 ounces of No. 7½ shot was fired. The chart indicates that this shell averages 395 pellets. Let us further assume that you counted 229 pellet holes in the circle of your paper target. Therefore, your percentage is 58. Your gun is, therefore, in the modified-to-improved-modified class, no matter what may be stamped on the barrel.

A far more practical reason for patterning your shotgun is to measure the actual distribution of the shot within the 30-inch circle. This is really the definition of "pattern." Should there be a concentration of holes in one area of the circle while other areas contain few pellet holes, or none at all, your shot pattern is poor, sometimes known as "blown." Switch to another brand of ammunition or try other loadings until you find the combination that patterns evenly throughout the circle.

"Gauge" in a shotgun means the same as "caliber" in a rifle or handgun but is indicated by rather antiquated means. This system was developed a long time ago by counting the number of lead balls of a specific diameter in a pound which can go through the bore of the gun. Let's try to simplify that a bit. A 20-gauge shotgun has a bore equal in diameter to a lead ball, 20 of which weigh one pound. All of the rest of the shotgun gauges are determined in the same manner. The only exception to this is the .410 bore. Its bore actually measures .410-inch in diameter.

These gauge designations are quite standard but not as uniformly standard as you might expect. The same gauge in shotguns made by varying manufacturers may differ in their diameter of bore as much as .025 inches. This is, of course, a very minor difference and shouldn't affect your choosing of a gun or its ammunition. But you should know that this discrepancy does exist.

The 12-gauge is, by far, the most popular shotgun in America today, with the 20-gauge the next closest in point of total number of shotguns and ammunition sold annually. The 12's popularity is due mainly to its combination of power, range, a recoil that doesn't cause undue punishment and availability of a wide choice of guns. One indication of the 12's popularity is the great number of places where the hunter can buy a box of shells for it should he run out of ammo.

At this point, a word of caution may be in order. Under no circumstances are you ever to use a large-gauge shell in a smaller gauge gun. In other words, placing a 12-gauge shell into a 20-gauge shotgun spells just one thing—disaster. The reverse—placing a 20-gauge shell into a 12-gauge gun—won't cause any problems. But the former will surely cause the barrel to burst with a good chance of injury to the shooter.

The really small gauges, such as the 28 and the .410, are often bought with the thought that they are ideal guns for women and young boys, especially beginners. There is no truth to this whatsoever. These gauges carry little knockout power on game in the field. True, they are light, easy to handle, and have somewhat reduced recoil compared to the more popular 12. However, the lack of recoil is a positive indication that the loads for these guns carry light powder charges. And, because of their scanty loads, they are fine guns only in the hands of skilled gun handlers who are superb marksmen, expert enough to use them only within their proper range limitations. In the hands of beginners, such guns are often disappointing in number of clean kills they produce. They are truly lightweights in every sense of the word, especially performance, when in less-than-expert hands.

The beginning shotgunner should start with at least a 20-gauge. If he finds the recoil a bit rough, he can make use of various mechanical recoil reducers as well as many types of butt pads. These, plus the use of reduced loads, make the 20-gauge a fine shotgun for the beginner. The beginner should also avoid too much test shooting of his new gun, especially at inanimate targets. Since the best method of firing for pattern is to take a rather large number of shots, the total effect of so much recoil may become unbearable for the newcomer to the sport of shotgunning. This may make him a bit wary of the gun. Such wariness could readily hamper what should be easy and casual use of the gun in the field. Therefore, it is more desirable that some experienced shooter do the bulk of the patterning job, with the neophyte doing most of his shooting at clay birds or other moving targets—and not to an excessive degree at any one period. This type of shooting, especially in the field, doesn't usually provide too many targets during any one day. This allows the beginner to take his shots without taking the chance that he may develop any "flinch," which would reduce his accuracy.

All advertising claims regarding shot shells should be taken for what they really are—means of promoting the sale of shotshells of a particular brand. After all, the manufacture of shotshell is a highly competitive business and the resultant product must be virtually identical in quality and performance at all price levels. Any refinement by one manufacturer is sure to be followed by all others. Hunters have their favorites—and that selection isn't always made in an intelligent or logical manner.

Some prefer red shells, other like green-colored shells. We're sure that were such shells available, there are others who would only buy multicolored shotshells. You'll probably fall into the same buying pattern, but the only true test of shotshell efficiency is how well it performs in a given shotgun—on a patterning board and in the field.

Some years ago, one of the manufacturers conducted extensive testing and found that at least 90 percent of all misses were attributable to insufficient leading of targets. Conversely, only 10 percent of such misses were caused by too much leading. These experiments consisted of painting life-sized targets on something similar to a conveyor belt and running it at varying speeds before a host of experts.

Based on these test results, the intelligent gunner will always give himself the benefit of any doubt about how much lead to give any target. When not positive, he will give his target more lead than he thinks necessary.

Because the average shotgun shot must be made hurriedly, the gun should be on the muzzle-light side for fastest possible target tracking. Therefore, the shotgun shooter's hands must be more flexible and stronger than the rifleman's. It is no mere coincidence that a shooter's performance suffers noticeably when his hands are tired and stiff after driving over rough roads on the way to the shooting grounds. Therefore, whenever possible, drive to your destination long before you start shooting so that your hands will be relaxed, rested and flexible.

Excessively long barrels on shotguns tend to tire the fore-end hand when shooting for a long stretch, are clumsy in the field, reduce the speed of the shooter's swing, and do not increase the shotgun's hitting power or the effective range. In other words, they serve no functional purpose whatsoever. They were a necessity back in the days of black powder to insure full combustion. The powder used in today's shotshells is comparatively fast-burning and reaches the all-burnt stage within 18 inches of barrel length. Beyond that point, the charge actually begins to lose velocity as the propelling power dies, but barrel friction continues. A shotgun with a 30-inch barrel emits a charge that is approximately 50 foot-seconds slower than one coming out of a 26-inch barrel.

Shotgun barrels of 30 to 32 inches are functional only when extreme-power magnum loads are being used. And then only when shooting in fixed blinds and for long-range use. Generally, a barrel of 26 to 28 inches is long enough to provide good pointing to insure fine pattern placement.

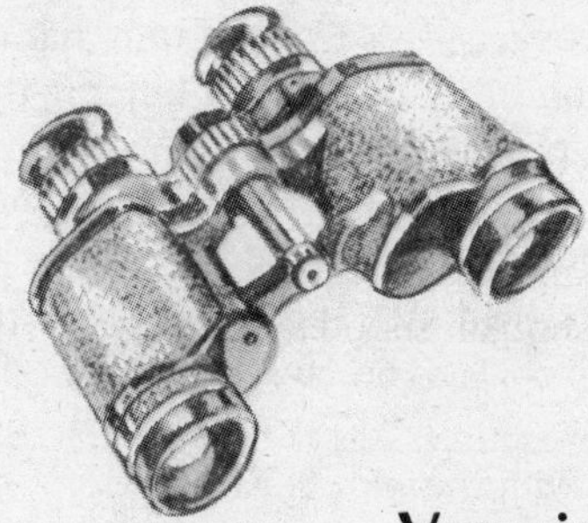

Chapter 15
Varminting Accessories

The items listed and described herewith can often mean the difference between success and failure in hunting varmints.

There is no sighting aid that can compare with a good scope for varmint hunting. These can be purchased with magnifications from 1X to 30X. However, remember that a shooter's ability to hold steady decreases markedly as the target is enlarged. For general field use, the average hunter can't be very accurate shooting with a greater than 4X magnification. A 6X can be used with accuracy provided that you shoot from a sitting or prone position and that you use a proper sling or have your elbows well anchored, either between your knees or to the ground.

Varmint shooting with an 8X or 12X scope is fine if a solid support is used. But it's highly questionable if a magnification over 12X will improve your performance. Also, the higher the magnification, the smaller is the viewing field. Therefore, the higher the power of scope magnification, the more difficult it is to hit a running target.

While there are many types of reticles available for scopes, the cross-hair varieties are best for varmint shooting. Variable scopes are particularly adaptable to varmint shooting since they are available in several combinations of magnification. With a variable scope, the rifleman can adjust to his needs of the moment. They are especially useful to the rifleman who hunts big game as well as varmints.

For the long-range varmint shooter, binoculars are practically a necessity. While it is true that some hunters rely on their scope to locate and identify their targets, it is likewise true that binoculars are far superior for this purpose. And you should buy the best binoculars you can afford. If you wear corrective spectacles, you will need a model with retractable eyecups. Most popular with varmint shooters are the 7x35 and the 8x30. Binoculars over 8X tend to be heavy and bulky and not quite suitable for hand-held use. There are some varmint shooters who favor wide-angle binoculars because they cover large areas of ground. However, it's sometimes difficult to pick out your target with the scope after spotting it with the wide-angle glasses.

For really long-range varmint hunting, a spotting scope is available. This can be useful when two men are shooting as a team. One of them watches where the bullets strike while the other is doing the shooting. However, it is unlikely that a hunter working alone will want to carry one far on foot because of its bulk and weight. Also, since the spotting scope has a high magnification power (15X to 60X), a steady rest of some kind is absolutely necessary. The field of view is relatively small and it is hard to locate a target, let alone hold the scope steady enough to see, unless you're using a tripod or some other sort of steady rest. Furthermore, the spotting scope can't be used hurriedly. And on a hot day, with the heat waves rising off the ground, high magnification merely aggravates the condition and makes it far more difficult to see your quarry. In summary, spotting scopes should only be used by teams of hunters working together, either in the sporting field or at the target range.

The man who hunts alone will find a range finder of value, especially if he doesn't shoot often and/or he is less than efficient at estimating distances.

Possibly the most revolutionary device added to the varminter's bag of tricks is the electronic game caller. Basically, it is a portable, battery-operated phonograph attached to an amplifier. Recordings of crow calls, authentic calls of rabbits in distress, etc. are readily available. They have definitely been proven highly successful in getting varmints into close range. For those who would rather do-it-themselves, there are a variety of manual calls. These are either mouth-operated or

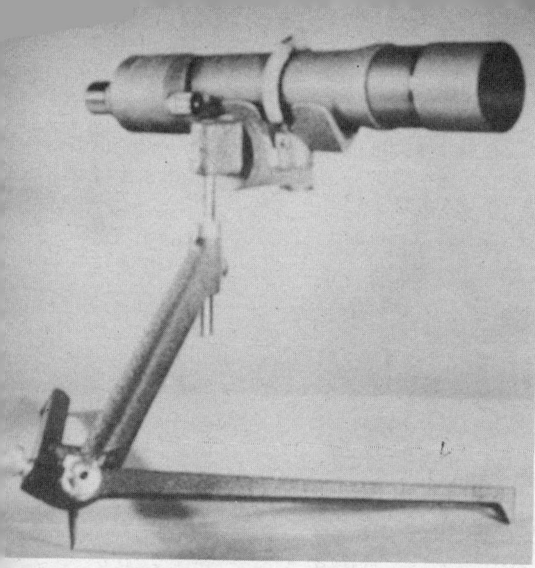

BALSCOPE SR. SPOTTING SCOPE (Bausch & Lomb)

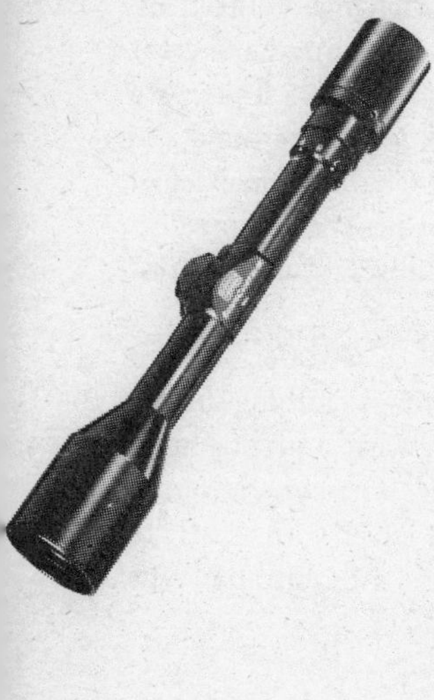

OLT

hand-operated. With a degree of practice, and listening to a phonograph recording, many hunters can imitate animal distress calls with surprising accuracy. Especially if they have a good ear for mimicry. The effectiveness of these calls has been proven so often that it can no longer be questioned. The results of this type of calling can be so successful as to seem uncanny.

If you're going out crow hunting, don't shortchange yourself by going out without decoys. Realistic, molded replicas of crows and great horned owls are available in most sporting goods stores. These are generally equipped with wire legs that can be stuck into the ground and also have a hole for attaching them to tree limbs. The combination of decoys and effective calling will be an attraction no crow can resist. These devices will bring the crows into shooting range . . . and the rest is up to you.

Last but certainly not least on the list of accessories varmint hunters, particularly crow hunters, need is camouflage clothing such as coat and pants or a parka. You should also either wear a netting hood or apply camouflage makeup to conceal your face. When you're out in open country where it is difficult to find natural cover with which to build a suitable blind, you can make good use of mosquito-bar type camouflage material.